About The Author

Lawrence Ray Mullen received his Masters of Social Work degree in 1987 at the University of Houston. He is also a Licensed Chemical Dependency Counselor (LCDC) and a Registered Sex Offender Treatment Provider for the Department of Criminal Justice (Parole Division).

It was the summer of 1966. I was twenty-five years old and had come to California filled with hope and excitement only slightly dampened by the Watts riots in progress. The radio played the song "What The World Needs Now Is Love, Sweet Love."

That was the Love that would light the road of the "new frontier," free of war and oppression, free of the life-stifling effects of authority. Had this not been the dream of all generations in history? The older generation had made a mess of everything and it was up to me and my generation to set things right.

The problem, I thought, was an oppressive, profit-driven, neo-fascist, militaristic "establishment" which fed off war and human exploitation. The problem was "Authority."

I had read the lines from Alexander Pope's "Essay On Criticism":

> A little learning is a dangerous thing;
> Drink deep, or taste not the Pierian spring:
> There shallow draughts intoxicate the brain,
> And drinking largely sobers us again.

I didn't realize at the time that Pope was describing me. As my "pride filled up all the mighty void of sense," I marched onward through the fog.

In the summer of 1976, I had come to the Texas State Hospital at Austin filled with despair and disappointment (only slightly alleviated by the seemingly distant promise of recovery in my arrival). The radio played the song "*Is That All There Is...*", a song which lit the road to nowhere.

The problem, I discovered, was my *attitude*. For over a decade I had led a life with little structure, few boundaries and as little deference to authority as possible. The freedom from authority which "the Age of Aquarius" had promised escaped as an evanescent illusion. I was like a man who had sought freedom from the law of gravity by jumping off a building.

I had lived a life run on self-will. That in turn led not to freedom but to enslavement to drug addiction and commitment to a mental hospital. I was a physical, mental and spiritual wreck.

In the Autumn of 1996, I had been free of drugs for twenty years. I had found a power greater than myself that had enabled me to live a happy and productive life.

In spite of all the disorder and despair I see in world today, I know millions of people in the United States and other places have found the power to live well. I believe this power lies within a person's ability to connect with a universal authority through living by spiritual principles or laws. I suspect the so-called "lunatic fringe" to which I was once so dedicated grows larger. The fringe now controls much of the government and society in general.

Only recently have I come to terms with having been an incest victim. That is why I have always had great dif-

Society
&
Sex
Offenders

by

Lawrence Ray Mullen, LMSW-ACP

Published by:
Emerald Ink Publishing
7141 Office City Drive
Suite 220
Houston, Texas 77087

(713) 643-9945
Fax (713) 643-1986
E-mail emerald@emeraldink.com
http://www.emeraldink.com

Printed and bound in the United States of America

Library of Congress Cataloging-in-Publication Data

Mullen, Lawrence Ray, 1939-
Society & sex offenders/ by Ray Mullen
p. cm.
Includes bibliographical references.
ISBN 1-885373-14-7

ficulty with intimate relationships. That is why I have never experienced a family life. That window in time has now passed and I have found peace with my fate. Knowing something was wrong represented the first step to recovery. After that, I had to know the *what* and the *why* of my fate.

I guess I always knew what had happened to me. For many decades of my life I simply ignored it, giving little thought to the consequences. When I finally acknowledged the truth, a flood of insightful and painful memories filled my mind. The illness poured out like the corruption from a great feverish cyst. As the pain subsided with its accompanying rage, the healing began.

I first began working with sex offenders professionally about ten years ago. Looking for ways to make a living, someone introduced me to a woman who operated a small sex offender counseling agency. Sometime later I set up my own practice.

I was surprised by the feeling of empathy I encountered in myself while working with the sex offenders. I had expected a situation where I would need to counter my feelings of resentment. Instead, I quickly connected with their humanity and was able to say "There, but by the grace of God, go I."

Although not all sexually abused children grow up to abuse others, almost all sexual abusers, I believe, were themselves abused as children. Interestingly, not all sexual abuse is legally recognized as abuse. Indeed, most sexual abuse may not be recognized at all.

For example, we recognize many of these following examples easily:

- a man calls his daughter names because of how she dresses;

- a woman engages her teenage son in a nonsexual spouse-like relationship.

These parents are sexually abusing their children, but breaking no laws.

What is my interest in writing this book? My interest originates out of both my personal and my professional experience with sex offenders. I have come to see the problem of sexual abuse as one branch on a great tree of family and social dysfunction. As in other branches of the tree of knowledge, we are currently addressing perhaps only a twig on that branch of dysfunction (and doing that with very limited success).

I believe that the degree of society's willingness to *own the problems*—to search for solutions, and to act on those solutions—will determine the ability of the United States to continue as a nation. My own personal experience tells me that this can be done.

Dedication

To Mabel

Some time ago a lady named Mabel died in a Los Angeles hospital. Mike said he didn't know what year. I hadn't seen or spoken to her since June of 1974 and I had wanted to find her, to thank her for telling me to go home to my people.

Mabel knew about going home to one's people, about connecting with the spirit, the spirit of the human community, the spirit of the life, perhaps the spirit of the universe. Mabel was a Luiseno, a Native American of California's Pacific Coast.

In 1974, the Native Americans of California seemed to be the only people in that state in touch with that sort of community. That lack of a sense of community may permeate the entire United States today.

The United States government had once sent Mabel to San Francisco to become a secretary. Following the long American tradition of trying to "solve" the "Indian problem," the Eisenhower administration decided to send young Native Americans to the cities for job skills training.

Mabel did dream of a better life. Her life instead became a living nightmare. There was nothing particularly wrong with San Francisco—she just didn't belong there. Finally, she returned home to finish out her days working among her people.

Mabel's shared much of her people's ways (which brought back memories of my great uncle's ranch in central Texas where scores of family would gather for the annual family reunion). That was just the one reunion. We still had two others to attend. We were family, we were America, we believed we were the children of a loving God, and that we would all be together in heaven some day.

In 1974 I couldn't really connect with what Mabel was trying to tell me but what I was doing wasn't working, so I went back home to Texas. Today I know that a spirit is working in my life. The spirit is not Texas and it is not my family, but those things appear to have helped me connect with that spirit.

The spirit—call it God or the spirit of the human community—can lift a person out of the mire of *self* into the boundary-free totality of a spiritual or god-centered universe.

Thank you, Mabel. May the spirit of your love live evermore. To you I dedicate this book.

My Aunt and Uncle

To a long-deceased aunt and uncle who introduced me to the topic of the sex offense, may God have mercy on their souls.

Table of Contents

The Scope of Sexual Abuse

In the United States at least *one in ten men* and *one in four women* are victims of sexual assault at some time in their lives. No one really knows how many for certain but the number is high.

In 1992 Nurun Shah, M.D. estimated that between forty and sixty percent of the adult patients admitted to the Harris County Psychiatric Center in Houston had been the victims of sexual assault at some time in their lives. Other psychiatric facilities around the country report similar findings.

With those figures in mind, the extreme public concern over sex crimes is not surprising. The sexual abuse devastates the victims, the victims' families and society in general. People are demanding action. They should be demanding action, demanding action to stop this violence.

The incidence of sexual crime is taking a terrible toll on child development. Much of the damage results from the abuse itself but damage also results from the extreme measures taken to protect potential victims.

Parents who once allowed their children to run and play—to experience life at its fullest—are becoming more and more watchful and protective. Terrified by the thought of harm coming to their most precious loved ones, they live in fear and mounting anger. Unfortunately, while protecting their children from predators, they may also cut the children off from many positive life experiences.

Restricted by their parents' fears, children themselves miss valuable contacts outside of the home. Adults who could provide them with needed learning experiences are often seen as potentially dangerous and to be avoided.

During a recent television interview, an elementary teacher stated she that was no longer willing to physically comfort a child for fear of being accused of sexual abuse. This degree of emotional neglect may be almost as damaging to children as sexual abuse.

The teacher had good reason to fear touching the child. Fear-driven public hysteria has led to the arrest of many seemingly innocent men and women across the country. Famous among these incidents was a "sex offender witch hunt" in Kern County, California which ended only when the children began accusing *prosecutors* of abusing them. Later, the accused were released as convictions were reversed. The assistant district attorney who spearheaded this miscarriage of justice was dismissed in disgrace. This prosecutor should have been himself prosecuted along with the police who cooperated with this destructive and dishonest assault on justice.

The falsely accused, the children who were dishonestly manipulated and deprived of their parents, and the entire justice system have been victimized. These political misuses of the criminal justice system makes the apprehension and prosecution of real abusers more and more difficult.

Children do not generally lie but they can be easily manipulated into believing something that is not true. Prosecutors and others with a personal or political agenda calling for convictions did tell the children things like, "This is what you need to say if you want to see your parents again." Dishonest and threatening interrogation is an ethically questionable tactic when used against an adult suspect. When used to get children to destroy their own families, the tactic is deplorable! If our criminal justice system is to work, honesty must take precedence over winning.

In spite of giving lip service to the presumption of innocence in criminal prosecution, many Americans appear to presume the guilt of any person charged with any crime. These faults in the criminal justice system as well as many of its strengths lie in its political nature. This is especially true of sex crimes.

In response to the sexual abuse problem, people are demanding that more and more offenders be apprehended and imprisoned for longer periods of time. Their demands are being met but in ways not being scrutinized closely by the public. The daily news screams of case after case of sexual assault. More and more, however, charges are being dropped and convictions overturned because of DNA testing and "victims" recanting their testimonies. This judicial irresponsibility may make it more difficult to prosecute real sex offenders in the future as the judicial system loses its credibility.

Seemingly, conviction and imprisonment do not impact the frequency of offenses. We currently imprison more people than any industrialized nation on earth except Russia. We have the largest number of convicted sex offenders on earth, yet offenders keep coming in record numbers.

Consider the following statistics.

Number Of Persons Incarcerated In 1993

Country	Per 100,000 People
Russia	558
United States	519
Union Of South Africa	368[1]
Canada	116
Great Britain	93
France	84
Germany	80
Netherlands	49
Japan	36

[1.] Statistics gathered prior to the advent of dramatic democratic reforms in South Africa culminating in the election of Mr. Nelson Mandela as president.

Sex Offenders Per 100,000 Population

Country	1993	1994
United States	81	76
Canada	45	48
Germany	31	--
France	--	29
Netherlands	26	--
Russia	11	10
Japan	2	2

Interpol Statistics 1993, 1994

One major problem with the *criminal justice solution* is that someone has to be victimized for it to be employed. There is no way to arrest and prosecute an offender until he or she victimizes someone. This is not to suggest that the criminal justice system be abandoned as a tool in fighting sex crimes. However, we may want to consider other solutions which might help arrest the problem *before* someone is hurt.

The great American poet-philosopher Ralph Waldo Emerson once said that for everyone striking at the roots of the problem there are a thousand striking at its branches. The roots of the sexual abuse problem in the United States are deeply intertwined in the sexual attitudes and practices of our country. Deeply, beyond the reach of the criminal justice system, the roots of sexual misconduct spread throughout the degenerating family and community systems of this country.

The incarceration of sex offenders is a major way of addressing the problem. While somewhat effective, this method can never be employed to an extent that would *solve* the problem. Therefore, we should explore other avenues of addressing the problem of sex offenders.

The criminal justice system largely strikes at the branches of evil rather than at its roots. Many American systems do this. The delivery of medical services, for example, focuses more on curing disease than on preventing of disease.

Our systems largely react to rather than prevent problems. Nevertheless, considerable segments of the criminal justice and medical systems focus on prevention. Prevention gains more and more public attention. The educational system represents the prime example of an institution dedicated almost entirely to the prevention of problems.

We can surmise that the central problem is a systemic one: a generalized national social dysfunction.

Sexual abuse and sexual dysfunction go hand in hand. Sexually dysfunctional people are both the abusers and the abused. The pathology passes down through family lines and festers in pathological community systems like bacteria in a petri dish. Statistical evidence of sexual dysfunction in the United States is found everywhere as the following statistical examples suggest:

Marriage/Divorce Rate per 1000

Country	Marriages	Divorces
U. S.	9.9	21.2
France	4.8	8.5
Canada	6.9	12.9
U. K.	6.9	12.9
Germany	6.1	8.3
Japan	5.9	5.1

Now let's look at children's well-being in different countries by examining the teenage pregnancy rate for every 1,000 women from ages 15 to 19. The following table includes both live births and abortions.

Teenage Pregnancy Rate per 1000 Women Ages 15-19 Circa 1983

Country	Pregnancies
U. S.	98
Canada	39
U. K.	45
Japan	10

We can examine the nature of children's well-being in other ways as well. What is the percentage of children in single parent families?

Percentage of Children in Single Parent Families

Country	1960	1980	1986
U.S.A.	9.1	19.7	23.4
Canada	Unknown	12.8	Unknown
U.K.	Unknown	12.0	14.0
Norway	Unknown	10.9	13.9
Sweden	7.8	13.5	Unknown

Notice that over twenty percent of American children live in single parent households. In some population groups, the percentage is well over fifty percent! Child development researchers have found that two healthy parents are needed for normal child development. It is widely believed that the presence of the male parent is important in the development of internal behavioral controls. The lack of male parenting in the United States may well be a factor in the tremendous increase in violence among young people.

Female parenting is equally important in child development in different ways. The overburdened single parent is limited in the ability to respond to the children's needs in any way. Even when child support comes, it seldom meets the economic needs of the family.

A century ago, single parent families were not usually an economic option. If something happened to one parent, children went to live with relatives (sometimes along with the single parent) or they were institutionalized. The extreme demands of earning a living by working twelve hours a day six days a week and even heavier work loads for the home maker made single parenthood impossible for the working person.

As I write this paragraph, I am doing the laundry. When my grandmother did the laundry, she had to chop wood, haul water, build a fire, make soap, scrub each item, rinse each item, hang each item to dry, and then iron the clothes with an iron heated on the top of wood stove. What takes me 15 minutes took her two days. I am waiting for the invention of a machine which will also gather up the clothes and fold them when they are finished. Of course, those which must be ironed go to the cleaners.

Economic progress and improvements in the status of all women and of working men have allowed the single parent family to survive in many cases but seldom to prosper.

Not all single parent households are headed by women but the majority are. A substantial and growing number of males head single parent families. These children are similarly deprived of the benefits of the functioning two parent household.

The degenerating American family system is the crucible in which criminality—including sexual assault—is being created. The loss of family structure and the loss of other values have been accompanied by and associated with the destruction of immediate community systems.

In the past, people generally belonged to large extended family systems. These families were in turn associated with small ethnic communities which served to define and enforce community standards of behavior.

Increases in productivity and mobility have largely destroyed the small human organizational structures of the past which have become less and less economically relevant.

The problem of sex crimes is *our* problem. Like it or not, sex offenders come from and are a part of our society. Like maggots from carrion, sex offenders are the product of the degenerating rotten American family and community systems. Dysfunctional systems are the products and the producers of much pathology including chemical dependency, violence, sexual deviancy and sexual assault.

The sexual revolution of the sixties and seventies promised to produce an age of sexual enlightenment. The sexual revolution instead produced an era of sexual indulgence and irresponsibility.

Recently, due to the murder of five year-old Jean Benet-Ramsey, Americans were introduced to the topic of child "beauty" contests. In these contests, small girls are exhibited as sex objects (surely to the delight of all pedophiles). This is only one example of the perverse way many people of our country view sex and the female person in particular. Probably without thinking about what they are doing, people are allowing their own children to be inadvertently exploited for the sexual gratification of pedophiles.

Another problem with the system is that it only targets the offender. The system rarely addresses the state of the family and community systems which produce offenders. In virtually all families of sex offenders, there are what I will call "co-offenders."

Frequently co-offenders are spouses of offenders who were themselves sexually abused as children. Their own painful experiences blind them from the truth and keep them in denial. They are unable to see the pathology in action. They have developed coping skills to live with the problem and not see it as abnormal or not see it at all. A typical co-offender would rather think their child is a liar than to believe that their spouse is an offender.

The sex offender also manipulates the victim to support the pathology. In this way they also become co-offenders. Many people are puzzled when an adult comes forth to claim they were sexually abused as a child. Many ask, "Why didn't they speak up sooner ?"

The reasons for the silence of the victims are quite complex. The victimizer instills a fear of exposure in the victim that is even greater than the fear of the sexual assault. In addition to fear, there is also confusion. Children naturally trust adults and they find it difficult to act against adults in their environment. They simply do not have the knowledge to evaluate the situation.

This fear of exposing the crime is not limited to the child victim. There is still a fear many adults (including men) have of being known as a victim of sexual abuse. In the Judeo-Christian tradition, women are largely blamed and certainly devalued after being sexually assaulted. The book of Deuteronomy in the common Bible calls for women to be put to death if they are raped in the city. This is still the case in some Moslem countries.

A woman I once treated was blamed by her parents when she reported a date rape. During treatment, she finally revealed this to her husband of twenty-five years. His acceptance and warm support facilitated her recovery. The fact that she would withhold this from her husband for so many years fearing his response is evidence of how deep the wounds of sexual abuse go. Abusers thrive on this vulnerability.

When an incestuous father tells a child he or she will be put in a terrible place if they tell, or when a pedophilic clergyman tells a child he or she will go to hell if they tell, the child tends to believe the adult. If the adult tells the child that they are the cause of their own pain, the child tends to believe this.

Sometimes the offending behavior is supported by a large extended family system. In such dysfunctional family systems the victim is either ignored or blamed for the situation. When and if the situation is brought to the attention of authorities, the victim is attacked as a betrayer, an enemy, by the family.

Until we find some way of addressing the problem of deteriorating family systems, the systems will continue to produce sexually and socially dysfunctional people. Dealing with the offender only does not get to the root of the problem.

In addition to our reliance on incarceration of the offender, we have also identified treatment as another method of addressing the sex offense problem. Almost all treatment is now focused on sex offenders who have completed their jail or prison sentences. The offenders are sentenced to treatment as a condition of probation or parole.

Rarely do people present themselves for treatment prior to offending. Almost as rare is the involvement of whole families in treatment. Even if successfully treated, the offender is frequently cast back into the same social sewer from which he or she came.

Current treatment efforts do not hold out the hope of making great changes in an offender's sexual makeup or other personality traits. As with those who have survived their victimization, the scars remain. The damage is permanent. Like their victims, sex offenders can learn to cope with life more effectively. They can develop skills to avoid re-offense but their basic personality and patterns of sexual behavior can never be totally or permanently changed.

Another failure of current treatment efforts is that, like the criminal justice system, treatment efforts only address the branches and not the roots of the problem. They treat the person only after he has become an offender, only after his patterns of behavior are set. If a way could be found to address the pathology in childhood, the offense behavior might be avoided all together.

In addition to our failure to intervene at an early age with the offender, we have developed pitifully few means of addressing the problem at the family and community systems level. We are still only striking at the branches of the evil and ignoring its roots.

In 1990, I began working with sex offenders. I hoped my efforts would reduce their offence behavior. My primary motive was to save as many victims as possibly. This is how sex offender treatment differs from other forms of treatment. The interests of society and the unknown, unseen, potential victims supersede those of the client.

While I had to consider the interests of society, I knew that I could not disassociate from the interests of the sex offenders and provide effective treatment. I had to acknowledge and connect with their humanity as well as that of their victims. In considering this problem I came upon the root concept I was seeking—the great tap root of what I am calling *spiritual communion*: the spiritual communion of all humanity.

As much as we may wish to disassociate from evil, evil is part of the human mix and it is within all of us. There is a little Adolph Hitler and Charles Manson in all of us no matter how Buddha-like or Christ-like we may aspire to be. If we deny this, we have lost the battle against it. The spiritual communion I speak of applies to the evil as well as to the good and we must acknowledge the evil to combat it.

My own Anglo-American ancestors were in many ways good Christian people but their virtue did not stop them from practicing genocide against native and Hispanic Americans. They did this to possess the land that they forced African slaves to work. If I were to go back one hundred and fifty years, my ancestors would be ready to show me exactly how their religion permitted them to do this. They could kill and enslave people because they believed the people they killed and enslaved were not really people worthy of their respect.

The people they killed and robbed were no better than the heathen idol-worshiping Canaanites whom God ordered Joshua to kill.

The Spanish were, of course, Christian, but they were Roman Catholics, and that was much worse than being idol-worshiping heathens to many Protestants, not that the Spanish treated native Americans with great Christian charity.

If you need to know where these people received their religious guidance, read the book of Joshua in the Judeo-Christian scriptures. For example:

> They devoted the city to the Lord and destroyed with the sword every living thing in it—men and women—young and old, cattle, sheep, and donkeys.
>
> *Joshua 6:21*

I asked an Israeli guide once how the Book of Joshua differed in spirit from Hitler's "Mein Kampf." His answer was that God had ordered the slaughter of the Canaanites and Hitler was not God.

Like the slave-owning genocidal societies of the past, our culture believes it can disassociate from the evil within by denying its human origins. We could continue to pretend sex offenders are not really people if we chose to do so, but in doing that we put the problem beyond our reach. We must see the human connection, the spiritual connectedness, to work towards solving the problem.

The first time I treated a married couple in an incest situation, I was unprepared for the wife's charge that "... that filthy little bitch (her ten year-old daughter) destroyed my marriage by coming on to him (her husband)."

The woman (I'll call her Mrs. Jones) was thirty-five when she married her then nineteen year-old husband. She herself had been sexually abused as a child. Have we really identified the offender here? Is it the husband, the wife, the wife's incestuous father? All of the above? Society's failure in this case is that it could find no way to intervene prior to the destruction of a child's life and subsequently many other lives.

The husband had done well in treatment. He had even obtained a vasectomy to prevent having any more children but he was still in the incestuous family system. Society had rightly held him responsible for the sexual assault of his step-daughter, and he *was* responsible. Society failed, however, in not recognizing the existence of the larger family system. This approach to solving the problem is like swatting mosquitoes in a back yard filled with pools of stagnant water. It is like surgically removing only part of a malignant tumor.

The remedy that society prescribed in the case of the Jones family addressed only a small part of the problem and in some rather bizarre ways. The brilliant minds of Children's Protective Services gave the children to the offender's *parents* to raise (in an unconscious preservation of the pathology for future generations).

The sexual abuse of children and others, like all social dysfunction, is a symptom of a deeply-rooted spiritual deficiency. That deficiency is the product of a social break in spiritual communion. Many people in this country are seeking spiritual answers to the problems of society and are working to establish or re-establish spiritual contacts. Millions appear to be doing this with success, if without much public notice. The simple, if not easy, requirement of gaining spiritual connections is found in the Biblical admonishment, "... seek and you shall find..."

The reality of the situation is that sex offenders, like street gangs, racists, murderers, drug addicts, butchers, bakers, candlestick makers, doctors, lawyers, Indian chiefs and saints are *us*. They are part of the human condition and they are supported in this condition, as all of us are, by families, communities, the nation and the entire world. As Walt Kelly's cartoon character Pogo once said, "We have met the enemy and the enemy is us."

This is not to say that most people approve of and actively support the behavior of sex offenders and other criminals. We do, however, as a nation inadvertently promote the conditions that foster such behavior in unconscious (if not conscious ways). Only to the extent that we acknowledge our responsibility for the problem can we have the power to solve it.

We rightly seek to assign blame to the offender. Sex offenders must be held responsible for their actions. In assigning this blame, we should not lose sight of the bigger problem, a systemic problem which goes far beyond the activities of the individual offender.

In the United States we fight the idea of social connectedness. We strongly believe in the *cult of the individual*, the self-made person, the individual unbound to his or her environment, independent, self-willed and totally responsible for what we are and what we do. Ironically this is the source of both our greatest strength and our greatest weakness.

The ancient Greeks referred to the strong self-reliance as *hubris* or excessive pride and self-reliance. It was a recurring theme in their tragic drama. Hubris always angered the gods. Even Solomon said, "Pride goes before a fall."

Our society tends toward compartmentalization to segregate problems and people. We like to think in terms such as the "sexual abuse problem", the "unemployment problem", "the problem of inflation", "the abortion problem" and so on.

Many do not tend to look at the systemic nature of things. Many do not sufficiently appreciate the reality that all creation is interrelated or connected. Our tendency to compartmentalize and divide is evident in every government form which asks us to identify ourselves by sex, race, religion, economic group, profession and other variations.

Most people go to great lengths to disassociate from those people who check the other boxes on government forms. Looking at things in this unrelated or disconnected way is like describing a human heart as a whole human. We compartmentalize, create artificial boundaries, and try to disassociate. Thus we flee and hide from responsibility.

The problem is that society can never be understood until we acknowledge the spiritual communion of all people, of all life and of all creation. The concept of the "heart" as an organ makes no sense outside of the context of the whole body and the body can not survive without the heart. The "sex offense problem" makes no sense when separated from the whole of the human community, no matter how much we may wish it did.

Sex offending is a systemic problem of enormous proportions. The sex offender is both the cause of and the result of that problem. We must find a way to treat sexual as well as other social dysfunctions as part of the whole if we are to make progress in reducing them. We must address the issue at the family and social levels if we are to make any progress in solving the problem.

We are discussing systems here. I do not wish to suggest that the individual sex offender is not responsible for his or her own behavior. These individuals should be held fully accountable for their crimes. I wish only to suggest that we should not and cannot stop at the point of punishing the offender if we wish to make progress in solving the problem.

Sexual dysfunction in society is as old as time and it is well-documented everywhere in ancient texts. There is probably no topic except perhaps the existence and meaning of a higher being which receives more historical attention than sex.

A number of references to sex occur in the Judeo-Christian religious writings. Most of them raise some interesting value questions.

In the greatest Biblical sex scandal of all, the cities of Sodom and Gomorrah were destroyed due to the sexual indiscretions of their people. According to the Book of Genesis, not even ten righteous men could be found in these cities. Finding ten righteous men could have saved Sodom according to God's conversations with Abraham.

Abraham was trying to cut a deal with God to save his nephew, Lot, who lived in Sodom.

Much is not said in the Bible. It is possible that Abraham was afraid Lot would come and live with him if rendered homeless by Sodom's destruction. Or perhaps Abraham was just trying to save Sodom. Who knows exactly why he pled so strongly for Sodom's salvation?

Lot, the one man saved from the destruction of Sodom, presents us with some rather unusual value questions. When the men of Sodom demanded sex with the two angels who had come to warn Lot, Lot offered them his two virgin daughters instead. Luckily for the girls, they were not wanted by the mob. In Lot's defense, he possibly knew his daughters were safe. The angels solved the problem by striking the lecherous mob blind.

Blindness is probably the least punishment anyone dumb enough to try to sexually assault an angel could expect. Of course, these visually-challenged sex fiends were blown up the next day with the rest of the city's inhabitants, all except for Lot and his family who fled to the mountains as directed by the angels.

As Sodom burned, Lot retreated to the mountains where the Bible says his daughters got him drunk and then snuck into his bed to get pregnant. They violated the only known universal sexual taboo: parent-child incest. If Lot was the most righteous man in Sodom, one wonders what those who perished must have been doing. The story reports that Lot was drunk and did not realize what he had done. Imagine the effectiveness of that defense in a sex offender trial today. Who would believe a man too drunk to recognize his own daughters could function sexually?

Lot's wife did not make it to the mountains. She disobeyed God's order not to look back as they fled. She was turned into a pillar of salt. According to some, this pillar remains today on the southwestern shores of the Dead Sea.

Since ancient times, sex and sexual dysfunction has been a reoccurring theme in history. It is a major theme in Greek mythology and in Rome. Petronius Arbiter satirized the sexual behavior of first century Romans in the "Satyricon." The "Satyricon" is so bawdy that complete English translations were banned in the English speaking world until well into the twentieth century.

Worldwide sexual standards of behavior have tended to go through cycles ranging from extreme license to extreme repression. Prior to 1950, a sort of hypocritical repression characterized the attitude of Americans towards sex. The 1940's were a time when sanitary napkins were wrapped in plain brown paper and stored behind the counter in drug stores. Only a few decades before that, pregnant women went into seclusion when they began to show. Pregnant teenagers at this time tended to disappear for a few months and their return was heralded by the miracle birth of a baby by their middle-aged mothers.

Prostitution flourished in the United States in the early twentieth century. The booming prosperity of houses of prostitution in the late nineteenth and early twentieth centuries belies the hypocritical front of chastity and sexual propriety claimed by the literature of that time.

In 1947, the Kinsey report on the sexual behavior of men and women in the United States was published. It blew a million holes in the fabric of social self-delusion and hypocrisy. Millions of Americans were delighted to find that many of their "deviant" behaviors were actually normal.

By 1960, modern contraceptives and antibiotics appeared to have eliminated the problems of disease and pregnancy. In 1973, the *Roe vs. Wade* decision introduced the option of the legal abortion. Prior to that, abortions were illegal but easily arranged. This included many dangerous and often deadly procedures by abortionists who were not physicians. They practiced in places where considerations like sanitation were not controlled.

In spite of the new information, sex education in high school of the fifties and even much later was usually provided by football coaches who showed horror films of third-stage syphilis and lives ruined by teenage pregnancy. They told teenagers this is what will happen to you if you have sex. Unfortunately, the teenagers' bodies had a different agenda, as always.

The new information did set the stage for the so-called "sexual revolution" of the 1960's and 70's. This agenda of this event was largely dictated by the hedonistic philosophies of "Playboy" and "Cosmopolitan" magazines. Much of the anti-free sex movement of the 1980's and 90's was being touted by the disabled veterans of this revolution as well as the religious right (which never participated in the sex, or, at least never participated openly).

Many Americans who lived in the 60's and 70's have concluded that the sexual revolution, like the Russian and most other revolutions, did not come off as well as expected. Revolutions often do a good job at tearing down the old systems but they usually do not result in the development of new functional systems—at least not immediately.

The French went about one hundred and fifty years after their revolution of the 1790's before they achieved any governmental stability for more than a couple of decades.

At this point we might note that "Playboy" and "Cosmopolitan" are still best sellers and there are still monarchists in France. The so called sexual revolution is anything but over. In spite of epidemics of unwanted pregnancies, antibiotic resistant sexually transmitted bacteria, AIDS and sexual violence, many people still view sex as simply a recreational activity.

A loss of respect for our sexuality has led to social chaos. Sex is a great source of power for both good and evil and the fantasy of modern men and women. That they can turn it into a trivial pursuit is at the root of the problem of sexual violence.

Uncontrolled sexual activity has led to and continues to lead to social disorganization, violence and disease. Sex is a powerful force. It is to be enjoyed, for sure, but also to be respected. In thinking about the power of sex, I am is reminded of the ancient Chinese metaphor of the person riding a tiger. How do we get off of the sex tiger and get it back into its cage?

One major reason for the confusion of modern times has been the extraordinary increase in human productivity and technological ability over the last century or so. Humans work half as much and live twice as long as they did in 1900. Women have achieved much freedom and are no longer viewed as the property of their fathers or husbands. Women have experienced the greatest change in social status over the last century and have many more life choices to ponder. This is true for men as well who have been freed of much of the drudgery of the past.

It is clear to most that the old system of doing things has gone by the way. People could not go back to the past even if they wanted to. We are not going to go back to the farm and reestablish our ethnic identities. Women are not going to submit themselves to their husband's authority and the barefoot, pregnant, and bread making roles of the past except maybe in Afghanistan.

It is also clear that no adequate rational, functional system of sexual and other social behaviors have been developed which might ensure the ability of men and women to sustain a relationship long enough for children to reach maturity. The successful raising of children is the only natural rationale for the family. It is up to Americans individually and within their communities to develop coping skills for the current and future age. If the children are not properly nurtured, there will be no future age.

These statements do not apply to everyone. There is a minority of functional families in this country and it can and will form the basis for the regeneration of the family system in whatever form it evolves.

Viewing sex crime as a symptom of social dysfunction is not a way of relieving sex offenders of the legal and moral responsibility for their crimes. It does put forth the idea that much can be done to prevent sex offense behavior by identifying and treating potential offenders in childhood. Although many children are sexually assaulted by strangers, most are the victims of people in their own families and immediate communities. Sex offenders within the family or immediate community and those who are strangers come, without exception, from dysfunctional family systems.

Sexual predators also come from sexually-dysfunctional family system. Robert Hazelwood, formerly of the F.B.I., has spent many years investigating and apprehending sexual predators. He says that he has never known a sexual predator to come from a normal family.

High-risk families that produce sex offenders and other criminals can and should be identified. This idea is nothing new or radical. In the past, tightly-knit communities monitored the functioning of families and intervened strongly to enforce community standards. We can restore this community function through our educational and other community systems.

Trained educators, clergy, and others in schools and religious institutions could identify the symptomatic distortions of thoughts and behaviors characteristic of affected children and develop interventions to help solve their problems. Families affected by the intervention will complain but they already complain when their grown offending children are led off to prison. Society has standards and these could and should be defined for all children in society. Deviant families were not tolerated in the communities of nineteenth century America and they need not be tolerated today.

Many say that it is better to cope with deviant behavior than to interfere with the freedom of families and individuals. This is not a trivial point and Americans have to make a decision as to what we want to do. Do we want unrestricted freedom at any costs?

Much of the controversy centers on the question of government intervention in the private lives of citizens. Social controls of the past were generally not implemented by the government, either national or local. They were implemented by immediate community social structures upon which individuals and families depended for support.

Others people reject the idea of community standards as a violation of minority rights. These people refer to the "cross-cultural perspective." All standards do not have to be universal. We have always been a diverse society with diverse standards and there is no need to change this. This does not mean we should throw out all standards for fear of offending someone or some group. In the past, people immigrating to the United States had to comply somewhat to different standards.

In the past, immigrant populations were generally allowed to set and enforce their own standards. They generally lived in their own ethnic communities, communities which have largely disappeared.

One great still intact ethnic community, Chinatown in San Francisco, continues to resist strongly any outside interference in its social order. In the 1960's when school integration became an issue, the citizens of San Francisco's Chinatown vigorously protested the idea of busing their children to schools outside of the community. They rightly felt their children would suffer from exposure to what the considered to be the diluted values of the general community.

Our criminal codes already define boundaries on behavior. Many standards are otherwise incorporated into the our social institutions. Can we all agree that pedophilia, incest, teenage pregnancy, sexually transmitted diseases, rape and family violence are not to be tolerated? Surprisingly, some people do not agree on even these items.

To some groups, a pregnant teenager means an extra welfare check. Many people believe some women deserve to be raped if they behave incorrectly. Others believe a man has a right to sex with his spouse with or without permission. Some believe it is alright to have more than one wife, and others believe a man should be able to inflict physical injury on a wife or child who displeases him.

A few years back, a woman in the Portuguese community of Boston was gang-raped in a bar. The general consensus in the Portuguese community was that she deserved this for being in the bar. They were furious when the rapists received long prison terms and the women had to leave town for her own safety.

The Portuguese of Boston are not unique in this belief. Blaming the victims of sexual assault is as old as history. Ancient Jewish law requires that a victim of rape be put to death if the rape occurs in town. Jews no longer do this. In some countries controlled by one of Judaism's daughter religions, Islam, rape victims continue to be severely punished, even killed.

We do not, as a society, have to tolerate deviant behavior if we do not wish to. If this becomes a matter of constitutional concern we can change the constitution. The Bill of Rights has not prevented society from outlawing certain behavior and there is no reason that it should now. We can and should attack those behaviors and their underlying value systems. We have the means. We need to act if we want a change.

We do not have to tolerate the intolerable behavior of deviant groups or even of some ethnic and religious minorities when their behavior violates the rights of others, including children. A judge recently sentenced a Cambodian to jail for eating a German shepherd. The judge's rationale for this was that this offended the sensibilities of Americans. How much more should the sensibilities of American be offended when a Moslem sends his daughter to Africa to be surgically mutilated?

American mythology, civil rights are not
ven. They are man-made. The original
ie civil rights outlined in the United States
Constitu... lave been greatly modified by the Supreme
Court and we need to address the effect of these modifications.

If the acts of the judicial system are found to be unacceptably socially destructive, constitutional amendments or even a constitutional convention might be in order. Even with legal constraints we can take action. Through our schools and other educational system, we can address at an early age when it will do some good the problem of sexual misconduct.

We now know that sex offenders begin to act out a very young ages even though this may or may not be identified as sexual misbehavior at the times. Of course, a seven or eight year old can not act out sexually as an adult but children will model the behaviors of adults in their environment. Children of ages three and four are often identified as victims of sexual abuse by exhibiting behaviors uncharacteristic of their ages. Many cases of sexual abuse have been identified when even very young children are observed sexually abusing other children. These children are acting out as instructed by adults in their environment.; they are also learning behaviors and attitudes that will follow them throughout life.

Rational sex education programs in our elementary schools could do much to reduce sexual misbehavior in later life. Understanding something about what it is to be a man or a woman and a parent, understanding proper sex roles, understanding the power and beauty of human reproduction, and understanding sexual responsibility are all lessons children can be taught. They can be taught the appropriate lessons at the appropriate age. Deciding what is appropriate is, of course, the issue.

Of the countries listed in the earlier statistics all except the United States and possibly Russia provide good sex education for young children. The results of our anti-sex education policies are clear. The United States has more than twice the teenage pregnancy of Canada and the United Kingdom and almost ten times that of Japan. In the Netherlands, the teenage pregnancy rate is virtually zero.

Two groups of people who vigorously oppose sex education are the religious right and pedophiles. Both, of course, have their own reasons for keeping children ignorant and confused but the results for children are the same. The religious right confuses children when they hypocritically tell adolescents to deny the reality of their hormone-driven sexual awakening. Children can not and will not ignore this development.

Many Americans don't know what to teach their children. Of course, sexually abusive parents don't want to teach their children the right lessons but most parents certainly do. The lessons for life passed down through our ancestors no longer seem to quite fit. They no longer quite fit because they do not quite address the needs of today's people.

Dramatic and rapid changes in the way men and women relate to each other have raised many new questions. Relationships which once were defined by male heads of household are now negotiated between men and women.

In the past, sexual choices for both men and women were severely limited. These were not only limited by social conventions but by economics which dictated rigorous sexually differentiated work schedules for survival. Men had to work twelve hour days, six days a week, and women worked even longer to maintain households. In 1900, people lived an average of forty years. There was no time for alternate life styles or multiple roles.

Choices and freedom are wonderful commodities. Certainly few, if any, moderns would be willing to sacrifice them even if this were possible. New choices, however, require the development of new coping and problem solving skills.

Ignorance about sex seems has been a national virtue for many in the United States. Until about fifty years ago, sex education for boys involved taking them to a house of prostitution in their teenage years. Girls learned to cook, clean, and sew and were told to do whatever their husbands who had been trained at the houses of prostitution told them to do. Many, if not most, men and women have given much thought to the development of their new roles and relationships and worked hard to developed the new problem-solving and coping skills called for by social change.

In spite of the complexities of modern life, a minority of good functional families tend to raise good functional children. Even if these families are becoming statistically rarer, many continue to exist as models. Perhaps the T.V. talk shows should try topics such as "parents whose children completed college," "parents whose children have never been arrested" or "parents of children who don't do drugs."

This book will suggest some solutions to today's problems but its main purpose is to encourage people to seek solutions to problems.

We will have to look away from the government and from big institutions for many of our answers. I believe if America is to survive the twenty first century it will do so because people have solved their own individual problems. America will change one person at a time. We will change one person at a time but in concert with others within a social order.

We somehow have to find a way to reconstitute an order in which we can function as individuals, as families. An order which can give us some guidance.

There are many problems in our society which call for our attention. On the positive side the United States Of America is a wonderful and exciting nation which has challenged the human heart, mind and spirit to the fullest. There has been little in human history as wondrous and glorious as the sight of the first person walking on the moon.

In the last century the United States and the rest of humanity has put an end to many of the diseases of the past, have virtually eliminated famine and real life-threatening poverty. We have doubled the life span of people in only one century and we have put a telescope into space. This telescope looks straight into the eyes of God straining to see the very beginnings of creation.

The beginning of the new millennium promises great wonders and many challenges. I believe our society must and will find a way to survive and prosper even though there are problems along the way to overcome. I believe we will do this by connecting with the power of our creation and/or creator.

We are a nation of dreamers, creators, and doers. We are also a nation of rebels. Our origin was that of English colonies which served to resettle rebellious and trouble-some religious minorities in English society.

Our rebelliousness is a source of great energy and creativity but within it also are the seeds to sow our own destruction. The human spirit is like the fire which cooks our food, keeps us warm, and propels our automobiles. It is also an energy source which can burn the house and the whole city down if not properly harnessed.

At this point I want to note that I have made some harsh comments about religion and other social institution. I did not do this to offend anyone although it surely will. Religion is a social institution fallible in its secular nature. If religion is to become and remain relevant in the lives of people, it must be willing to face the truth and work to correct its internal problems. I believe have said nothing in this book that is not well documented.

In spite of their problems I believe the religious institutions of the world provide mankind with a guide to future progress that is ready and willing to be accessed. It is vital to acknowledge the great value and well as the limits of religion in a search for progress.

I believe that the United States and the rest of the world are moving to meet the challenges of the twenty-first century. For Americans as elsewhere this challenge includes the development of family and social systems which will appropriately meet the needs of people in the future.

A country which can go to the moon should be able to solve its sex problems. Well, maybe. Perhaps space travel is less problematic than sexual relationships.

Defining The Sex Offender

Some people think of the "sex offender" as a sort of generic sub-human creature that will attack anyone and anything. Others see the sex offender as simply immoral and out of control. Still others imagine a person who is mentally ill. In actuality, the term sex offender has no clinical meaning (or even any real legal meaning). It refers to someone who has been convicted of an illegal sex act.

The people we refer to as "sex offender" come in many specific forms and we have to know something about these many forms to develop realistic ways of controlling the problems they present.

First, it is vital to acknowledge that sex offenders, like all criminals, are human. They are a part of us as a population and we are related to them. To try to disassociate from them, isolate them, and even destroy them will not solve the problem. If we were to apprehend and put away all sex offenders tomorrow, our sexually dysfunctional society would simply replace them in a few years. The family and community system from which they originated will continue to produce the same results.

Sex offenders themselves are prisoners of patterns of sexual thoughts and behaviors that most of them desperately wish they could change. Most sex offenders do not really want to hurt anyone and certainly most of them do not wish to spend time in prison. They wish they could follow another path.

Some sex offenders are so lost in the pathology that they believe they are right and society is wrong. An example of this is the National Men-Boy Love Association (NAMBLA). This dreadful organization is dedicated to the promotion of homosexual pedophilia as a positive socially beneficial activity.

The men of NAMBLA refer to ancient Greeks like Socrates who wrote of sexual affairs with adolescent boys. They ignore the fact that the ancient Greeks executed anyone who sexually assaulted a prepubescent child. Members of NAMBLA mostly assault pre-pubescent boys. They are what is know clinically as exclusive pedophiles who can only respond sexually to children, not adults or adolescents.

Fortunately, the members of NAMBLA are the exception and not the rule and we should consider ways of eliminating such people from society for the safety of the children. There is no way such offenders will respond positively to treatment.

The only way the exclusive pedophile can avoid offending is to forego sex their entire lives and this is virtually impossible. No matter how much they may try to avoid the high risk situation, they eventually find children in their path.

The men in NAMBLA and others with such grave prognoses for change are not to be blamed for being what they are. No one can be blamed. They must be held responsible for their behavior, however, and children must be protected from their sexual assaults even though it means putting the offenders in prison or putting them to death.

There are those who say that sexual patterns of behavior are a matter of choice. These are like the people who say alcoholics drink simply because they want to drink. Their views are a mean-spirited, ignorant and counterproductive fiction. The people who say this are usually, and oddly, adherents of a religion that calls for love, understanding and acceptance rather than hatred, judgement and persecution.

This book seeks understanding, not bigotry, as a prerequisite to solving social problems.

The notion that a sexually dysfunctional life style is one that a person would choose over normal thought and behavior patterns is ludicrous. No one wants to have a deviant pattern of sexual behavior particularly when that pattern leads to ridicule, persecution, and, in the case of the offender, imprisonment. Most sex offenders deeply regret the life their sexual patterns have forced upon them.

Blind striking out in ignorance at the problem does not correct it. It only exacerbates it by causing more problems. Certainly one can cure cancer by killing the victim. One can also identify the nature of the cancer, and apply specific treatments, and seek to save the victim. If we try the latter course with sex offenders, we may make some progress in solving the problem.

Knowledge—not prejudice, ignorance and superstition—is the power by which humans are endowed to solve problems. Oddly, many humans frequently have an aversion to rational thought. They turn instead to violent emotional reactions in a effort to solve their problems.

Those who claim people can change their sexual orientation through self-will generally call for imprisonment and other punishment of the sex offender as the only answer to the problem. Ironically, their claim supports the myth that all sex offenders can benefit from treatment. Many, unfortunately, probably cannot. We do not need to hate these offenders but we do need to keep them away from potential victims.

A person's sexual patterns of thought and behavior are set at some age and are extremely resistant to change. The person can learn new skills which can help cope with their behavior and avoid re-offense but the original patterns are essentially set forever in the personality.

Our myths about sexual behavior based on simple ideas of good and evil and self-will do not and cannot help us solve the problem of sexual abuse. We need to develop social systems responsive to the reality of sexual behavior if we are to make headway in doing this. Mostly, we need to seek ways of reaching the thousands of children who are growing up to be sex offenders. *The average sex offender first offends in early adolescence, not as an adult.*

By the time society addresses the problem (largely through the criminal justice system), it is too late. The damage has already been done. Lives, sometimes many lives, have been affected in terrible ways.

We have the resources to research the problem, gain knowledge and develop alternative approaches to solutions. When and if the current witch hunt frenzy abates, society may be able to approach the matter of sexual abuse in more rational and productive ways.

Both the federal and state governments are currently involved in passing a barrage of legislation which promises to do little more than convince constituents that something is being done to protect them. Most of this legislation is just smoke and mirrors.

Sex offenders need to be dealt with. The sexual abuse of children and others must be stopped. To do this, we need to learn more about who and what we are dealing with. People who can not be rehabilitated by prison and/

or treatment need to stay locked up; the benefit of any doubt about their prognosis should be on the side of the victim.

The Legal Perspective

The phrase "sex offender" is a loosely termed phrase of convenience used by journalists and others within the criminal justice system. It is a loose classification given to a number of persons who have committed an offense related to sex. The different legal definitions given sex offenders are behavioral based in the most simplistic terms. These definitions vary depending on the nature of the act or acts, and who the victim is or whether or not there *is* a victim. The definitions also vary from state to state and country to country.

The initial legal charge for a sex offense does not necessarily provide a good description of what happened from a clinical point of view. By the time the charged offender goes through legal processes like plea bargaining, the nature of the offense may be totally obscured. The courts are not designed to diagnose sexual behavior. They are designed to try to administer justice.

All states have laws against sex acts committed by adults against children and non-consenting adults. These include *rape* or *sexual assault* as well as *indecent exposure*, *indecent acts*, and *sexual harassment.*

State laws differ in minor ways but most in the United States have similar provisions. Penalties vary considerably in different states, but trend towards greater severity in all states.

In addition to laws involving non-consenting adults, laws exist against sex between consenting adults. Homosexual acts are illegal in much of the United States, but these laws are rarely if ever enforced (except when the acts are committed in public). This would be generally the same for heterosexual acts committed in public. The term *in public* would include places open to the public such as adult sexually oriented businesses. Unless such public acts are committed in the presence of children or non-consenting adults, they could be viewed as crimes without victims.

In addition to laws protecting children from adults, all states also have laws concerning sexual acts involving children. In general, the laws consider the age of majority as eighteen. All states have laws prohibiting sex with pre-pubescent children. Criminal laws involving sex between adolescents vary considerably.

In some states, the law defines an absolute *age of consent*. Some provide for legal consenting sex between adolescents and other adolescents or adults up to a certain age. An age differential of two to five years is common. Some states treat adolescents as children in sex crimes. In Texas, for example, an eighteen-year old who has sex with a fifteen-year old may be charged with sexual assault of a child. Oddly, that same eighteen year old in Texas can marry the fifteen year old with parental permission.

Most will agree that adolescents need protection from sexual activity but how much protection and from whom remain debatable.

Obviously an adolescent raped by another adolescent or adult experiences great trauma, as would an adult, but what about the adolescent who consents? The law in some states says an adolescent cannot give consent to a sex act. Laws of this type reflect a legal, not a social or clinical, reality.

In ancient times, the *puberty rite* marked a person's passage into adulthood. The Jewish *Bar Mitzvah* or *Bat Mitzvah* is a relic of this but it no longer allows the initiated participant to function as a adult in society. The rite does retain a religious significance as well as a social significance in a more limited way.

Much sexual abuse of children is *not* illegal. Laws regarding sexual abuse are focused on physical acts committed mostly by men. I recently interviewed a pedophile who presented his relationship with his mother as normal and uneventful. When pressed, he admitted that they experienced one conflict. When he was thirteen, his mother remarried and he had to sleep somewhere else. His mother had not touched him sexually; she had broken no laws but she had inflicted severe emotional damage on her son by violating incest taboos. Society needs to look at this if the problem is to be solved.

how?

In short, much (if not most) sexual abuse involves interpersonal interactions that do not include overt sexual activity such as that associated with sexual intercourse and the law has not found a way to address this.

In this case, the man, is the mother responsible for her son's sex offense behavior? Certainly not. Is she responsible for his pathology? Absolutely.

A mother who referred to her ten-year old daughter as that "slut who ruined my marriage" broke no laws in saying what she said but inflicted perhaps more damage on her daughter than the incestuous father. In another case, a mother lived with six different abusive men, two of whom sexually abused the children. The mother would be viewed by society as one of the victims but her behavior put her children in a situation where they were victimized.

In still another situation, a couple blamed their teenage daughter for causing the *date rape* she had suffered. These parents broke no laws, but in blaming, they blocked their daughter's recovery. They inflicted more damage than the rapist. Years later (after much psychotherapy), this lady confided in her husband of twenty-five years. She had feared he would blame her as well, but his warm support of her lifted her out of her insanity.

The father who calls his daughter a slut commits no violation of the law, but his verbal abuse may do almost as much damage as an illegal physical assault.

If society could find a way to have the law address the full spectrum of sexual abuse and other forms of abuse within the family and larger social systems, we would have a more effective tool in preventing sexual assault.

Family of origin issues are not an excuse for sexual assault but they are the reason the pathology develops. Men do not grow to adulthood and just decide to be pedophiles or rapists. They are raised to be what they are.

We must learn to look at *sexual assault* as merely one aspect of the general sexual dysfunction of society. We must look at if as one of the branches of the evil if we are to truly understand it and find solutions.

The Clinical Perspective

The clinical view of sex offenders is very different from that of the legal system. No such thing as a "sex offender" exists in clinical terminology. Some sex offenders have no clinical condition and some sexually very disturbed individuals commit no illegal acts.

An eighteen-year old who is having a sexual affair with a fifteen-year old is a sex offender in many states. The eighteen-year old may be breaking the law but the behavior between the two may be quite normal. Their behavior may involve poor judgement and it may involve breaking the law but it is not necessarily the result of any pathological condition.

This is not to say that society has erred in attempting to protect adolescents from sexual activity. In today's world, a fifteen-year old is not generally mature enough to become a parent or be involved in an adult sexual relationship.

In the case of rape, we deal clinically with both the rapist motivated by sexual gratification and the rapist motivated by the sadistic desire to inflict pain and terror. The first of these two can respond to treatment. The prognosis of the second is extremely grave. There is virtually no hope for successful treatment of the sadistic rapist.

The law does not generally distinguish between the two types of rapists unless the sadistic rapist actually inflicts physical injury. Of course, the victim may find it difficult to appreciate the distinction between the two as *all* rape inflicts pain and terror, regardless of the motivation.

The important distinction here is that some rapists can change to become people who will not re-offend and some cannot change.

In determining effective measures to employ on sex offenders, the law needs to make a distinction between the sadistic rapist and the one motivated by sexual gratification. It needs to deal differently with the two. The sadistic rapist should be imprisoned for life or put to death to protect others in society.

Short prison terms, probation, parole and treatment of the sadistic rapist are a waste of time and money. They also pave the way to further and progressively more violent victimization of others. These ineffective measures also allow the sadistic rapist to return to the community where he will surely re-offend.

The law also does not distinguish between the *exclusive pedophile* and the *non-exclusive pedophile*. In many states the law does not distinguish between sex acts involving a pre-pubescent child or those involving an adolescent. Clinically, this distinction is critical. The exclusive pedophile, virtually 100% certain of re-offending, is allowed to remain in the community.

The exclusive pedophile can only respond sexually to pre-pubescent children. To avoid offending, they must lead sex-free lives. There is no hope of them engaging in satisfying sexual relations with adults. Non-exclusive pedophiles can respond sexually to adults; this ability to respond can be developed.

Like the prognosis of the sadistic rapist, the prognosis of the exclusive pedophile is so grave that they should be imprisoned for life or put to death. This sounds draconian. However, the lives of children are simply too precious to be put at risk on the perhaps thousand-to-one odds that these people will not re-offend.

As a clinician (a sex offender treatment provider), I deeply wish I could be more optimistic about exclusive pedophiles, sadistic rapists and other sex offenders. Treating sex offenders is how I make my living. If I can help a sex offender live better, fine, but my primary motive is to protect future victims, to prevent re-offense. This is how sex offender treatment differs from most other treatment modalities. The unknown victim is always the primary consideration.

The need to protect children should have top priority. I believe the state and federal legislators feel the same way. Sending sex offenders to treatment and making them pay for it is a low-cost option only when you do not figure in the priceless value of the welfare the victims.

Only the public can force public officials to pass laws which would keep certain sex offenders behind bars. The public, of course, must be willing to pay the price of doing this.

Politicians give lip service to solutions but pass laws which do little to solve the problem. Neighborhood notification, commitment of sex offenders to mental institutions, referring sex offenders to treatment with no consideration of their diagnosis and prognosis, posting pictures of sex offenders in public parks, are all easily implemented, low-cost measures. These measures do little or nothing to solve the problems.

To utilize the clinical solution effectively we must be willing to honestly admit to its limits. Clinicians are under pressure by the criminal justice system to claim to produce results. Judges, probation officers and parole officers usually do not like to hear about poor prognoses. This contradicts their claims of having done something positive by referring an offender for treatment.

Perhaps someday we will develop techniques to help all sex offenders alter their thought and behavior patterns but we are now nowhere near that.

We also define sex offenders in terms of their predatory nature (as opposed to opportunistic nature). The opportunistic offender, we assume, will offend only if a victim exists in his or her immediate environment—victims known to them personally. The predatory offender will seek out victims.

Once a sex offender has been referred for treatment, the diagnosis is often quite difficult. Many if not most sex offenders develop highly sophisticated social skills to mask their activities. They frequently employ these social skills in engaging others to participate in their cover. For example, many exclusive and non-exclusive pedophiles are able to live with and marry adult spouses who will meet their needs for cover or even provide them with victims in the form of children or grandchildren.

These spouses (usually but not always women) may or may not expect a sexual relationship. Not all people consider a sexual relation as a necessary or even desirable part of a marriage. They are often the products of incestuous or otherwise sexually dysfunctional family system.

A number of diagnostic aids exist. Among them are the polygraph examination, The American Psychiatric Association's Diagnostic Criteria (DSM-IV), family and personal histories and criminal history.

A carefully designed polygraph examination is the best way to uncover the thought as well as the behavioral patterns of the sex offender. The examiner must break through denial and obtain statements from the offender.

I recently referred an incestuous father for a polygraph. I believed this offender to be a low-risk non-exclusive opportunistic offender. The polygraph revealed an extensive history of sexual predation showing him to be of high risk of re-offense with a much poorer prognosis.

Exclusive pedophiles can learn coping skills to avoid and reduce the re-offense risk but these skills have a limited value. The chance of avoiding re-offense permanently is virtually nil. Many exclusive pedophiles are so frustrated that they develop elaborate thinking errors to justify their sexual activity. Society naturally finds these thinking errors to be offensive.

Although I am a sex offender treatment provider, I have dark thoughts when I hear a sex offender explain how he was seduced by a child. He will tell you this because this is what he actually saw happening. He is not lying. He really believes what he is saying. These thought distortions, the most terrifying aspect of the offense behavior patterns, may be eventually acted out.

Recently, I arrived at the local parole office to do a group and found one of the sex offenders in the waiting room talking to a child. When I asked the receptionist why a child was speaking with a pedophile in the waiting room, the entire place immediately mobilized to separate the two. It was like I had stepped on an ant mound.

The pedophile explained that he liked to talk to children because they were accepting, understanding and non-judgmental. Actually, most people like talking to children for much the same reasons but most people do not see the child's attention as an invitation for sex. The pedophile had lost his right to speak with children because he does think of them as sex objects.

Everyone knew that this young man liked to talk to the boy because he found him sexually attractive, everyone except the young man who was caught in his own denial and rationalization. That he was involved in this behavior in the waiting room of the parole office clearly demonstrates that he was not in touch with his own motives.

Denial and rationalization appear in other ways as well: in teaching children to act. Children can be taught to act out in a pseudo-sexual way by sex offenders. This is not real sex to the child. It is a child doing what an adult tells or shows him or her to do. The child simply wants to comply, to please the adult. Only the pedophile sees a child's sexualized behavior as sexual on the part of the child. When a pedophile is confronted by a child who has been taught to act out in a sexual way, he imagines that the child wants to have sex.

One of my clients brought his wife and seven-year old granddaughter by to introduce them. He thought if I saw his "healthy" granddaughter I would feel less pessimistic about his prognosis. To show me how healthy she was, he had dressed her in a dress that looked like it had been designed for a twenty year old tart and then shrunk to fit. She was wearing perfume and very carefully applied lipstick, eye makeup and jewelry.

After speaking with the offender about what I was seeing, I spoke to his probation officer and Child Protective Service. They got court orders keeping both him and his wife away from the child. The thought of that child actually brings me to tears. I can still see her innocent eyes shining because she had pleased her grandfather by "getting pretty" or "fixed up" or whatever he called it. He was shocked that his attempt to impress me in a positive way only offended me and several public officials. He desperately needed to be shocked.

One of the most shocking aspects of the preceding story was the subsequent complaint of the child's mother over the ban on visitation. The child's mother was also a member of an incestuous family system and had been carefully trained not to see the problem. She herself had been a victim.

I thought of the child when I saw the pictures of the Benet-Ramsey child and found out about the children's beauty contests. I knew there were contests involving children such as spelling bees but I had never known such beauty queen perversity existed. I imagine that just about every pedophile in the country has copies of the Benet-Ramsey child's picture. Her picture, dressed that way, is child pornography.

Many generally considered innocent things sexually stimulate pedophiles. Not long ago, a probation officer called me after a house search. We discussed how videos of children's movies, kittens and some women's magazines could be inappropriate in this man's environment. When the probation officer arrived, a children's movie played on the VCR while a litter of kittens caught the attention of a small child who was peering in the front door.

Many popular magazine are full of pictures of children; some without clothing. Some are printed for children. To a normal adult, these pictures are cute—good advertizing for products. To the pedophile, a child's picture, especially that of a partially nude child, is pornography. Some years during a search of pedophiles' prison lockers, an ad of the child with a dog pulling down his or her pants was the most popular piece of pornography found.

We have already mentioned a national organization of homosexual pedophiles known as the National Man-Boy Love Association. These men can not be convinced that young boys have no sexual interest in them. They even assert that this activity is good for the children's development. They are doing all they can to convince a horrified public of the benefits to society of this behavior. And also discussed was the need to identify exclusive pedophiles and to give life in prison or the death penalty for offenses for the protection of the nation's children. As with the sadistic rapist, short prison terms, probation, parole and treatment are a waste of time and money, at best only delaying the victimization of other children.

Most other sex offender can respond to clinical intervention, though no clinical intervention can guarantee 100% success. The earlier a sex offender can be identified clinically and treated, the better the treatment results.

Today, sex offenders are identified only after the are caught victimizing someone. An offender may have victimized dozens of innocent people prior to being caught. In almost all cases, sex offender behavior can be identified at an early age. Society can look for ways to identify early offender behavior and provide remedial interventions to solve the problem.

If we can identify the sex offender in childhood and provide treatment, we can circumvent the victimization of innocents and the great expense of relying on the criminal justice solution.

With the current legal system, someone has to be hurt to activate it. Many more people will have their lives ruined if we continue to depend only on the criminal justice solution. Rather than waiting to incarcerate sex offenders, we should intervene earlier, if possible.

The American Psychiatric Association's Diagnostic Criteria (DSM-IV) lists exhibitionism, fetishism, frotteurism, pedophilia, sexual masochism, sexual sadism, transvestic fetishism, voyeurism and paraphilia in its list of "paraphilias" or pathological sexual behaviors. As with most psychiatric diagnostic schemes, these represent only a crude understanding of human sexual behaviors.

The paraphilias listed in the DSM-IV do not all describe illegal activity and none are illegal unless acted out. Many sex offenses are not listed as paraphilias such as rape and sex with adolescents.

In the DSM-IV, the term pedophilia applies only to sexual ideation and behavior involving pre pubescent children. The law does not recognize the right of adolescents to consent and frequently does not distinguish between adolescents and younger children. The difference clinically can be quite profound for both the victim and the offender.

The prognosis differential between a man or women who offends with prepubescent children and one who offends with an adolescent is generally quite pronounced. The latter has more hope of changing his or her behavior. The law does not usually look at this difference and continues to refer the dangerous exclusive pedophiles for treatment in the community. Exclusive pedophiles are those who have a sexual response only to pre pubescent children.

While society's knowledge is severely limited we do know enough to start making some differential judgements about sex offenders. We could and should say that anyone who sexually abuses a pre pubescent child must be imprisoned for life without parole on the first offense. There is no need to place an additional child or a dozen children at risk going through the motions of giving a sex offender a "second (or third or forth or fifth) chance".

In addition to defining the pathologies of individual sex offenders we need to look at the family systems which generate and maintain these pathologies. Our legal and other social systems have very limited tools for doing this.

When men sexually abuse their children they frequently have the passive and/or active participation of their spouses. Spouses are carefully selected who will either look the other way or actually support the offense behavior. This spousal support is rarely viewed as criminal and after the arrest of the offender the spouse is free to repeat the pattern.

Frequently the spouse is herself a victim of childhood sexual abuse and is blind to the offense pattern by a denial dictated by their own experience. I am speaking as if the offender is always a man and the co-offender is virtually always a woman. There are a few exceptions to this but that is generally the case.

There is probably no way the normal mother of a child could be blind to her child's sexual abuse. At age fifty-five I could call my mother and she could hear a headache over the phone. Mothers—and sometimes fathers— are incredibly sensitive to the health and welfare of their children. A way should be found to force the participating spouses of incestuous pedophiles into treatment as well. They are as involved as the abusers but their involvement is seldom acknowledged by the law.

We do not look closely at the full spectrum of sexuality in formulating laws to control sexual behavior. The law does not look at associated thought patterns at all and generally only considers physical acts directed by men at individuals the law chooses to protect. When women are convicted of sex offenses, it is only when they actually have a physical sexual encounter with an adolescent and this is rare.

We do not really look closely at the behavior of co-offenders, those who support the abusive behavior. We give little consideration to how much it contributes to the problem. We look at the behavior of the offender and seldom go beyond that. Men and women can inflict severe sexual abuse on children and other adults without violating the law. To solve the problem we need to greatly widen our definitions of sexual abuse.

A Systemic View

If we wish to begin solving the problem of sexual offenders in society, we need to look at sexual assault in all its systemic manifestations. Even if we could catch all the sex offenders tomorrow and imprison them for life, we would have a new group of them in less than twenty years. Our society would make them like the underground roots of bamboo make new shoots no matter how many times we cut down the growth above the ground. In this chapter, we will explore the problem of sexual abuse at the level of the individual, family, community and larger social systems.

Our society wants to isolate the sex offender. We want to see the offender as only an individual, separate and different from the rest of us. We want to dissociate from the sex offender and pretend that he or she is some sort of alien unrelated presence. Some believe that we could solve the problem if we could only lock up all sex offenders.

Unfortunately, dissociation from sex offenders does not work. People may feel better to deny the humanity of sex offenders but the offenders, like all other criminals, are human. They are part of human society. They are us. Denial of this reality precludes the formulation of real solutions to the problem.

To begin solving the problem society, has to acknowledge that *we* are a nation of sexually dysfunctional people living in a sexually dysfunctional social system that *we* created. Sex offenders are simply those members of the system who act out in ways defined as criminal.

Society locks up sex offenders after the damage is done. Unless we address the social conditions which create them, more and more offenders will emerge to deal with. Society does not currently accept full responsibility for the problem. We punish the individual offenders we catch. We imprison them. We persecute them. We send them for treatment. We inform their neighbors of where they live. We raid their houses at night. In doing this, we generally overlook and ignore the real origins of the problem.

There is nothing wrong with punishing the sex offender. This is a legitimate and necessary approach to the problem of sexual assault. *The real problem is that we will do little to improve the situation in the long run if we stop here,* where we strike only at the branches of the problem and we need also to attend to its roots.

Almost anyone who alludes to the offender's family or larger social system as a source of the offense thoughts and/or behaviors will encounter quick and loud criticizm for trying to excuse the offender's behavior. Most people do not want to acknowledge their part in the problem.

I once spoke of the incestuous family system as a breeding ground for sex offenders at a group where I was shouted down by a woman yelling that family cause was no excuse. This woman identified herself as a victim of incest which occurred between the ages of nine and thirteen. She did not wish to look at either her mother's part in the crime or at her own inability to be other than a victim as part of the problem. She did not want to look beyond the individual sex offender for a manifestation of the problem.

In one way, the woman was right. There is no legal or moral excuse for committing a sex offense. She is right in saying that the sex offender must be held fully responsible for the behavior. If the woman's mother had been able to recognize the problem and intervene earlier, the damage could have been minimized. When the woman finally reported the abuse to the mother, the woman was accused of lying about her father. The refusal of the mother to acknowledge her daughter's victimization may have done as much damage as the sexual assault itself but neither the woman nor her mother (certainly not the law) chose to look at this aspect of the problem.

Spousal compliance is a necessary element in incest. The incestuous parent cannot function without this compliance. We need to fully acknowledge this resource of the offender to begin solving the problem. Today it is considered politically incorrect by some to "blame the victim." It is of course not necessary to blame the victim but we must acknowledge the responsibility, if any, of the victims in facilitating the commission of the offense.

Had the child been able to tell someone what was happening during the four years involved, the damage could have been minimized. Both the child and her mother were unable to act to change the situation. Even if they had acted, chances are that society still would have taken no action. Another very real aspect of taking action against the offender is that it will destroy the family system. The offender may be the family bread-winner.

The woman was wrong in another way, however. She was not interested in understanding. She was not interested in a real solution. All she wanted was revenge—to vent her rage—for the suffering she had experienced as a child. She did not want to hear about possible methods of prevention, methods (had they been available)which may have prevented her suffering in the first place. Worse still, she did not wish to view herself as a person in need of help as a result of the experience. She did not see herself as a person needing treatment or counseling of any kind.

Explaining the origins of behavior and excusing it are quite different. Excusing the behavior is a legal defense. Explaining it is a clinical, and humane, way of understanding the problem. Understanding problems is a prerequisite to solving them. Unless we begin to try understanding the problem in all its systemic manifestation, we will never begin to solve it.

Besides wanting to isolate the sex offender, we also isolate problems and try to address them outside of the context of the whole. Sexual assault, divorce, drug addiction and other problems are all symptoms of the same problem: the degeneration of the American family and other social systems.

Punishing the sex offender unfortunately remedies the problem only after the damage has been done, after someone has been victimized, after the offender is set in his pathology. This happens usually only after the offender is an adult and stuck in a set pattern of behavior. How much better would it have been to identify the offender in childhood and successfully treat or educate him? Both the offender and the victim could have been saved (at a fraction of the monetary cost as well).

Family systems and larger social systems produce, foster and protect sex offenders. In most cases, this support is passive and involves looking the other way. In some systems, attempts to cover up and hide or deny the reality of the situation comprise the passive support. Today, few people look rationally at the problem of sexual abuse.

Society is striking out blindly at the sexual abuse. Even those who would advocate a rational approach strike blindly at the problem. In seventeenth century Salem, Massachusetts, many of those who denied the existence of witchcraft and pled for a stop to the slaughter were themselves killed.

Today's largely irrational assault on the problem of sex offenders exhibits in many ways the mentality of a witch hunt or lynch mob. In fairness to the public, the terror of having one's children harmed does not call for a rational response, but we can solve the problem only by rational means.

The Individual

Currently, dealing with the individual sex offender remains the society's focus: apprehending, prosecuting, punishing, treating and controlling the offender. There is nothing wrong with this approach *per se*. No one I know argues for abandoning or even pulling back from it. Common sense and our social philosophy dictate that we hold the offender responsible for his behavior. Our social philosophy fails us, most Americans, inour believ that people have the absolute power to change their behavior. We cling to the myth that the pedophile, if sufficiently threatened, will become celibate or seek appropriate sexual gratification with adults. Antisocial behavior would not exist if people had the ability to change it. Try to tell this to the average person on the street. Belief in self-determination runs deep but the belief has severe limits. Against the demonic force of the sex drive, self-will is about as effective as it is on diarrhea.

Most people act as if the power exists to change individuals and that this power is easily and absolutely accessible. They assert that a religious experience or some sort of therapy can in all cases provide relief. Many people in fact find the power to eliminate undesirable behaviors. In 1976, the people of Alcoholics Anonymous estimated the recovery of over one million alcoholics in the organization. This number has obviously increased greatly in the last twenty years. Still, unrecovered alcoholics far outnumber the sober one, some say by a factor of ten to one (and different types of alcoholics complicate the picture as with the different types of sex offenders). Prior to the establishment of Alcoholics Anonymous, however, there were virtually no recovering alcoholics.

The book *Alcoholics Anonymous* asserts that no human power exists that will relieve one of alcoholism. Is this true also of deviant sexual behavior? With help, many sex offenders can reduce or eliminate their offense behavior, provided they recognize the problem, are determined to change, and can access the power to do so.

Sex offender treatment providers have identified some predictors of re-offense risk for sex offenders. To my knowledge, no one can honestly predict long-term absence of re-offence in any sex offender. In spite of some advances in our knowledge of human behavior, psychology, psychiatry and other social sciences are still elevated little from things like witchcraft and astrology.

Sex offender treatment can provide some benefits. Offenders can develop coping skills to avoid re-offense. These skills may be employed piecemeal to avoid offense behavior; in fact, treatment probably does substantially reduce the numbers of sex crimes.

Many in society would like to believe (many pretend to believe) that sexual offender treatment providers can work on sex offenders with the precision of an orthopedic surgeon. We barely have any idea of what we are dealing with.

The idea that we are dealing with the sex offender in a significantly effective way through treatment is a myth perpetrated by offenders who want probation or parole, by the treatment providers who want to make a living, and by the government which wants to dispose of sex offenders in an inexpensive way. Many individual sex offenders on probation or parole are far too dangerous to be out of prison. Even worse, many more have never been caught and continue to offend with impunity.

The Family System and Sex Offenders

The smallest and most basic social unit is the family. It may consist of as few as two people. Traditionally, the basic family unit consisted of a man and woman united by a religious and/or secular arrangement or contract. This unit provided for the creation and raising of children in a loving, provident and secure environment.

The family is the basic repository of all human behavior patterns, good and bad. The personalities of children are molded by their experiences in school, and society in general, but the main source of this developmental process is the home.

Clinically, sexual development cannot be separated from mental, physical, emotional and spiritual development as a whole. When we refer to such phrases as mental vs. physical, emotional vs. spiritual, nature vs. nurture, we superimpose a fiction of division in the human personality in order to define our concepts of the human personality. In reality, the human personality is an incredibly complex, integrated reality of which we have only a very limited understanding. We do understand something about the effect of some experiences on the developing personality.

One of the earliest realizations of the developmental needs of children was inadvertently noted in the state of Prussia in the eighteenth century. Anxious to free women for work in the manufacture of military armaments, the King of Prussia, Frederick the Great, set up massive day care centers with just enough staff to change and feed the infants in their care. After a short time, these physically and emotionally deprived children began to die so the project was halted. The children needed to be held, talked to, and otherwise stimulated to develop normally. The king reluctantly sent their mothers home to do this. Dead babies could not grow up to be soldiers and mothers of soldiers.

We only partly understand the effect of parenting on sexual development. Sexual differentiation on a social level begins at birth. Studies have shown that at birth new parents immediately engage in sexually-differentiated treatment of their children. This differential treatment depends on the sex of both the child and the parent. It occurs even with parents who consider themselves quite progressive and committed to equal treatment of the sexes.

Studies have also shown that such pathologies as alcoholism, physical abuse and incest tend to be passed down through generations of the same families. No matter how much a person may wish to be different, the strength of the parental model is profound. Naturally, positive values and behaviors are passed on as well.

Families tend to replicate themselves through their children. *Sexually abused children often grown up either to be sexual abusers or to marry sexual abusers*, participating in the abuse in more passive ways.

Not long ago I was trying to place a twelve-year old sex offender who came from an incestuous family of origin. At the boy's request, I called an uncle in another state who said he would be glad to take the boy if it was alright with the local child welfare and Adult Supervision and Correction agencies. When I checked with the agencies, I found the uncle was on probation for the sexual abuse of this same child. I also found out that every adult male in the family had a record of sexually abusing one or more children.

The breakdown of order in the family system is the major cause of sexual misbehavior. Robert Hazelwood, former F.B.I. agent specializing in the investigation of sadistic rapists, and Dr. William Pithers, director of Vermont's pioneering correctional sex offender treatment program, both say that they know of no sex offenders with a normal family of origin.

Referring the sex offender for treatment and ignoring the family system and family patterns will meet with very limited success. This concept should also be considered when designing conditions of probation and/or parole.

I recently worked with a man who had had relationships with five women, all with daughters from ages six to eight. He had been convicted of abusing only one of these children. At my suggestion, the court amended his conditions of probation to prevent such future relationships.

When I work with incestuous offenders I require family sessions during the treatment. The family cannot be required to come in for treatment, but it can usually be persuaded to come in as a requirement of a successful discharge. The offender has the option of terminating the relationship if the family refuses to cooperate. In these family sessions, the family pathology comes into full focus. Spouses of the offenders blame the *victim*, even when the victim is their own child or sibling. If they blamed the *offender*, they would probably no longer be married. Sex offenders have a natural ability to seek out spouses who will tolerate and even support or cooperate in the offense behavior.

One way of addressing the family system's role in sexual abuse is to hold participating family members responsible for their behavior. While their behavior is seldom prosecutable, their complicity with the offender's behavior probably is. This would enable the system to mandate family treatment and greatly enhance treatment in general.

The Immediate Community and the Sex Offender

The immediate community in conjunction with the family form the taproot of American society. In the past, several communities may have existed in one place, overlapping but highly segregated. When I was a child in San Antonio, most members of the Roman Catholic *religious community* were also members of *ethnic communities*. I recall a downtown church which was unofficially divided into four sections based on the English, Spanish, German and Czech languages. Marriage between people of different ethnic groups was rare. Marriage between Roman Catholics and Protestants and between Christians and Jews were also uncommon. This was true of communities throughout the United States at that time.

As the twentieth century progressed, transportation and changing economic conditions promoted the breakup of ethnic communities. Small, closely tied agricultural and urban communities based on ethnic or religious ties have virtually disappeared. Communities have broken up, their members scattered to the four winds. Mixed race, ethnicity, and religion are no longer barriers to marriage in the United States as they were only a few years ago.

In my typical suburban neighborhood live Protestants, Catholics, Jews, Moslems, Buddhists, Hindus, Anglos, Afro-Americans, Hispanics, Czechs, Pakistanis, Indians and Thais. This sort of mix is more typical of modern urban and suburban America than any sort of ethnic homogeneity. A few ethnic enclaves continue to exist. San Francisco's Chinatown is an example of this. Also the *reservation* arrangement continues to preserve Native American ethnic enclaves. These exceptions, however, are few. Small rural American communities are disappearing, along with the family farms of the past. Most consolidated into large agribusinesses. The distinction between rural and urban blurred. Modern transportation and communications enabled corporate America to disperse throughout the countryside and into smaller cities everywhere.

The need for massive corporate centers such as New York City, Chicago, and London lessens daily. People with computers can access an international communications network in a few moments and can do this in their pajamas while eating breakfast in the Rocky Mountains, the Caribbean, the Swiss Alps, or anywhere else there are phone lines.

Small ethnic communities were the keepers of values. Federal and state governments had little to do with questions of personal morality. Of course there were state and federal laws against theft, murder, rape and other crimes but enforcement of these laws and influence of community values were largely left up to the local forces.

As we learned during the civil rights movement, local white juries frequently frustrated the federal government in its early attempts to enforce change in the American South. Ironically, strong church-centered communities of Afro-Americans in the southern United States provided a spiritual quality of life and a power to effect change which was probably far stronger than that of the Justice Department and Congress.

In the old ethnic communities, individuals and families who refused or who were unable to comply with community standards of behavior could not survive, socially or economically. There were no federally funded state welfare programs to prop up the dysfunctional as we have today. Individuals and families had to be a part of the community or nothing at all.

Economics also dictated much human behavior. The simple economic demands on individuals were almost overwhelming. Much lower productivity at home and in the work place required twelve hour days and six day weeks of back-breaking work. The simple task of doing the laundry took two long days. Today machines do it in a couple of hours and involve little actual work.

The immediate economic dependency between the individual and the family and between the family and the immediate community has diminished considerably. Greatly increased productivity, aided by advances in communications, transportation and other technological areas have largely "liberated" individuals from the economic "ties that bind." At the same time, technological advances produced some wonderful results. We can travel and move about with a freedom our ancestors could only dream of. As you place a musical compact disc on your stereo, think of how once people had to wait for and pay dearly to hear music only at live performances. Not only can you access this in a moment but you have access to the best performers on earth and to an almost perfect technically manipulated performance.

In addition to other technological advances, medical science has doubled our life expectancy from about forty to eighty years in the last century. This gives us approximately seventy-five hundred additional days to enjoy life.

The price of all this progress is that we have largely been cut off from the spiritual and social structure of the communities upon which we once depended. Technology alone cannot meet the needs of the spirit; we have not yet found a way to meet these newly developed needs. Developing and accessing a spiritual framework for living is the challenge of today. This challenge is being met by millions of people.

Many places house a violent reaction to progress. In some Moslem countries, religious fanatics have sought to turn back the clock. In Afghanistan, women with doctor's degrees have been forced to return home and make bread and babies. This is in a country which desperately needs all the skills it can recruit to pull itself out of the dark ages.

On one hand millions are searching for new ways to access a spiritual framework by which to live. Other millions characterized by the so-called "fundamentalist" Moslems of the Middle-East and Christian "right" of the American Midwest and South seek to reinstate what they imagine to be past forms.

Whatever the outcome of mankind's search for spiritual structure, the result must include a way of proscribing boundaries on sexual behavior. As long as history has been recorded, the need to control the human libido has been recognized.

Past forms of community structure have not always provided a positive influence. The Archdiocese of Dallas-Ft. Worth has just been successfully sued for $120,000,000 for not acting appropriately to control a pedophile priest. One sexually abused altar boy was sufficiently disturbed to commit suicide. Other testimony came from a man who as a boy took showers with a priest who told him he had turned the water into holy water.

If this weren't enough, the bishop followed the judgment with a statement blaming the victims and the parents. Sexual deviancy will continue as long as the Roman Catholic Church continues to allow itself to be used for the employment of sexual deviates under the guise of "clerical celibacy." This problem was pointed out by reformationist Martin Luther five hundred years ago. This is not to suggest that all priests are pedophiles or that the clergy of other religions are without sin, but the jury in Dallas identified a systemic pattern of support for the behavior of the offenders as opposed to the welfare of the children.

We can find many other examples of community involvement in the perpetuation of sexual abuse. About ten years ago a teenage stepdaughter of a prominent citizen in a small American town shot her stepfather four times. He had been sexually assaulting her and she had spent months seeking help. The entire community, including her mother, refused to believe the truth. A local women's shelter refused assistance because she was underage. The police and child welfare agencies she approached simply called the stepfather to inform him of her activities. Only after the attempted murder did the community, and the child's mother, wake up.

Americans generally do not like to look at and intervene in the case of individual, family, and community behavior. The concept of boundaries—of restrictions—on human behavior is almost un-American. We are a nation of rebels. We are the nation where the phrase, "a man's home is his castle" was coined. This rebelliousness is reflected in international statistics.

The United States has twice the divorce rate of Europe and four times that of Japan. Twice as many children live in single parent homes in the United States compared to Europe. For our population, we have three times the number of sex offenders found in Europe and thirty-eight times the number found in Japan. The choice is simple. We have to live with this mess or clean it up.

We may have to rethink some of our ideas about personal freedom if we wish to change some of the statistics. Perhaps we will decide that more restrictions on individual behavior makes for too high a price to pay for a less problematic social order.

Macrosystems and the Sex Offender

State and Federal governments have somewhat crudely attempted to fill the void left by the demise of the community in American life. Some claim they helped create the void by reducing the dependency of people on the family and local community systems through public assistance and other support programs.

The government has established a vast network of assistance programs to aid people in need. These programs include social security, public assistance, food stamps and commodities, S.S.I., Medicaid, Medicare, Veteran's benefits, educational assistance and other programs. In addition to public assistance, direct subsidies, grants, government loans and manipulation of the federal tax system have imposed numerous pressures on society.

One criticism of government assistance asserts that it lessens human dependency on family and the local community and frustrates social attempts to set and enforce standards of behavior.

The government cannot begin to meet most of the social and spiritual needs of the immediate communities of the past. Even if it wanted to, it is too distant and its methods too crude to achieve a positive effect. Many people maintain that governments have facilitated the breakup of families and communities by promoting a dependence on public assistance as opposed to a dependency on family and immediate communities.

One government institution which addresses issues related to sex offenses is the United States Supreme Court. Though somewhat distant in its effect, the Court does make decisions which affect the lives of individuals. The decisions of the Court are not always positive in their effect. The court's recent decision to allow sex offenders to be committed on mental health warrants, regardless of their mental status, marked a new low in the functioning of this generally respected institution.

Internationally, women's rights groups have sought to address some issues effecting the welfare of women. To this end women convened the rather ill thought-out Women's Conference in China in 1995. Besides having to cope with the undisguised hostility of the Chinese government, women of the Third World and the West clashed over matters of priority. In many countries, women dreamed of having the right to vote or even survive beyond their child-bearing years. In the West, equal pay for equal work was a typical issue. In the West, methods of reducing crimes against women such as rape were an issue. In Pakistan, women who have been raped frequently have their noses cut off. In much of the Third World women are not only blamed for being raped, they are severely punished. Moslem fanatics have seized control of several countries. Women have essentially disappeared from the public, social and economic systems of these countries. In Afghanistan western-educated women, physicians, scientists, teachers, and others have been ordered to cover up, go home and make bread and babies.

On July 22, 1997, Reuters reported that Afghan women had been ordered to avoid making noise with their shoes when they walk. One can only guess at the sexually deviant ideation that led to this order.

It should be troubling to the citizens of the United States to know that their taxes were used to support the Moslem extremists of Afghanistan against both the Russian-supported Communists and the few in Afghanistan who wanted a democracy. Some of the arms we gave to these tyrants found their way to Iran and were used against our own troops in the Persian Gulf.

Some international issues have been identified and are being promoted by groups such as Amnesty, Incorporated and other civil rights groups. Currently, such groups are organizing a strong international effort to outlaw the surgical mutilation of baby girls in some Moslem countries. This process, known as female circumcision, is designed to prevent the enjoyment of sex by women. Egyptian attempts to outlaw this practice were struck down by the Egyptian Courts as they were seen as an interference with religious practice.

Why would people of such strong religious convictions express such displeasure in the way God created women?

Another problem faced the women's convention—the absurd geographical choice of China. This incredibly oppressive military dictatorship hardly seemed an appropriate meeting place for the free exchange of ideas. The choice of China for the women's convention does underline the immense arrogance of people in the western democracies who probably fantasized that their descent on China would be met with a sort of great democratic flowering of that nation. Instead, the Chinese considered this group too loose for the capital so they were moved from Peking to a dusty back-country hamlet where they would be less disruptive.

In view of the sexual chaos of the West, especially the United States, and in view of the barbaric conditions of most of the Third World, any sort of international solution to the world's sexual or other social problems is doubtful. People can and should continue, however, to bring enlightenment and civility into the world. May the spiritually bright (if secularly weak) voice of reformers continue to bring light to the darkness.

The Victim

While this book is essentially about sex offenders it focuses on the systemic manifestations of the problem rather than the individual offenders. Victims of sexual assault are an incredibly important systemic manifestation of the problem as a whole. Many sex offenders are themselves victims of sexual assault and both offenders and victims are products of family and community systems which generate the basic pathologies involved in sexual misconduct.

One thing common to all victims of sexual abuse is that they suffer profoundly from the experience. Somehow sexual assault touches the human spirit in ways which block out the joy of life and ravages the very soul of the victim. Victims general experience severe symptoms of dysfunction all of their lives. No one who experiences being sexually assaulted as a child can experience normal sexual development after that.

Sexual assault is extremely traumatic because of the importance people place on their sexuality, their sexual identity. No one knows exactly why human sexuality is a matter of such grave import but there are some strong clues.

The nature of sexual reproduction would seem to dictate this. Sex is the way humans procreate and the act of procreation requires a system for nurturing human offspring for the many years it takes them to mature and care for themselves. In other words, it is a serious matter.

Sexual reproduction is the only way we have of reproducing and enhancing the gene pool at the same time. While cross breeding, inherent in sexual reproduction, keeps the gene pool healthy, sexual contact between individuals also affords the occasion for the spread of infections. In addition to the spread of infection, sexual relations call for a maximum stressful effort in maintaining relationships. Everyone who has been married for any period of time knows something of the effort it takes to maintain the relation. This is an effort the divorce rate indicates few today are willing to undertake.

Throughout history mankind has assigned a high priority to systems of control over sexual behavior. Humans accomplish this primarily by laws and customs. The sexual behavior of other animals is naturally monitored. Everywhere other creatures which reproduce sexually do so in accordance with strict natural boundaries on behavior.

Generally throughout history human sexual behavior has been strictly controlled. Widespread sexual misconduct has generally been associated with the decline of a social order. Only domesticated cats and dogs tend to get a little out of control at times and this is probably due to their long association with humans.

With the onset of the so called "sexual revolution" of the sixties humans seemed free of some constraints. Contraceptives and antibiotics appeared to promise an end to sexually transmitted disease and unwanted pregnancy. The United States now has both in record amounts. In addition the United States has become the incest, rape, and child abuse center of the developed world. The sexual revolution, like the Russian revolution, promised much more good than it delivered.

I mentioned earlier that sex is a serious matter. This no longer appears to be the case for many in the United States. Perhaps I should say that many in the United States have deluded themselves in to believing that they can escape the seriousness and responsibility of their sexuality. More and more people appear to be waking up to the perils of unrestricted sex.

In the last few decades sex has been touted by many to be little more than a recreational activity. Unfortunately the manuals of this philosophy, "Playboy", "Cosmopolitan" and "Hustler" magazines are still at the top in circulation.

Even during the "sexual revolution" restraints on sexual behavior did not altogether disappear. Penalties for sexual assault on children and adults were greatly reduced, however, and this situation has undoubtedly encouraged the behavior.

The results of the destruction of boundaries on sexual behavior speak for themselves in the statistically validated destruction of family life in the United States. Prior to the "sexual revolution" after World War II, sex was generally and hypocritically viewed in the United States as a evil and base activity tolerable only because it was necessary for procreation. The main evidence of hypocrisy lay in the booming prostitution industry.

One bizarre sect, the Shakers, abandoned sex altogether. They finally died out as they could not find enough converts to replenish their ranks.

It is not surprising that the "sexual revolution" has been such a mess. Americans have never enjoyed a very healthy attitude towards sex.

Too many Americans tend to gather around the deviant extremes of the "Playboy" or "Hustler" philosophy on one hand and the denial and hypocrisy of the religious right on the other. These views treat sex on one hand as a sport and on the other hand as a base activity necessary for procreation only. Neither view presents a healthy pragmatic guide for young people in our society. Neither view has any basis in reality.

Developing a healthy and pragmatic view of sex is a prerequisite for reducing sexual offenses. The problem is that few Americans have a clear idea of what is normal in the area of sex, even if it is acknowledged as a powerful force for good and evil.

At this point it is important to say there is a great core of functional sexuality in the United States. Many individuals and families do quite well although they receive little press or media attention. This functional core will ultimately provide the seeds of our social recovery.

In addition to learned ideas regarding sex, adolescents are jolted by the onset of sexual hormone production. These children are told, if indirectly, by the sexual sport group to engage in irresponsible behavior, to follow their urges without restraint. Television, periodicals, and movies all treat sex in an irresponsible fashion in many cases.

On the other hand the religious right tells adolescents to ignore their sexual urges until they are married. Neither view gives children a way by which they can successfully live in the real world.

Associated with the importance nature assigns to sex, humans, from an early age, are conditioned to view their sexuality as highly personal and under their individual control. We call our genitalia "private parts" and children are taught from about age one or two to cover them up. Everyone has witnessed the parental intervention of a two year-old gleefully streaking nude in front of company.

By the time a child in the United States is three or four, being seen without clothes would be a source of great embarrassment. This is not universal and children in many societies are allowed to go without clothes. Nudity is not associated with sex in some societies as it is in ours. In a few societies even adults do not clothe themselves. In such societies however the privacy of one's sexuality is still honored in ways proscribed by those in the society.

In Western society, or more specifically the Judeo-Christian, nudity is view as sexual. This began with the story of Adam and Eve who covered their nakedness after eating the fruit of the tree of the knowledge of good and evil. Among many Jewish and Moslem sects maximum coverage of the human body, both male and female, is mandatory.

Whether very young children have a natural aversion to sexual activities by adults or are taught this, very young victims of sexual assault are aware that something terribly wrong is happening even if no physical injury is involved.

In addition to violating the sanctity of one's sexuality, sexual abuse also violates what I will call one's right to sanctuary in our homes and other private places. Burglars, robbers, and other criminals commit the same violations but nothing accomplishes this more than sexual assault.

Consider the plight of the child sexually abused by someone in the home. Every person has a need, a right I believe, to feel safe in the home. This is especially true for children. Home is everything to the child and a place of sanctuary to an adult as well. A child who is sexually or otherwise abused by a family member has no place on earth to hide; to feel safe. For the sexually abused the most intimate place in their lives has been violated.

Adults get a feeling of insecurity when their homes have been burglarized. We all have an illusion of safety and security in our homes. Burglars take that away when they enter our homes at will and do what they wish.

A friend recently shared with me that the worst part of having his house burglarized was that the thieves made sandwiches and left a mess in the kitchen. It was not so much the property loss but the loss of sanctuary, of that feeling of safety in the home, that had done the psychological damage. How much more does a victim lose when someone violates his or her own body ?

Fear of victimization haunts children and adults who have been violated. It haunts them their entire life. Most, if not all, women live in fear of being attacked at some time or another. This is especially true of those who have suffered an assault. Men are at risk but generally are able to deny much of the danger. Men are, in fact, less likely to be attacked, especially in ways which make them feel helpless.

Of course men sexually abused as children do not enjoy the feeling of security available to most men. All children and adults have a right to feel safe in society. To be able to go to a mall, to school, to a public park or anywhere. However we do not feel safe. People especially have a right to feel safe in the privacy of their own homes. In some ways the law does acknowledge this need. Burglary of a habitation, for example, generally calls for greater punishment than burglary of businesses. Perhaps the law should go further in promoting this safety.

Feelings of safety and security have been greatly com-
promised in the United States. The days when doors
remained unlocked and when children could play unhin-
dered throughout the community are gone, possibly forever.

When I returned from a trip to Jerusalem someone
asked me if I had been afraid of terrorists. Terrorists in
Jerusalem do not generally attack foreign tourists and
common criminals hardly exist there. I was caught across
town by sundown on Friday and as the sun went down
Jerusalem shut down. I walked several miles back to the
hotel and felt perfectly safe. Citizens in most cities of the
developed western world and in Japan can feel secure
walking their city streets at night. We in the United States
can too if we wish to make the changes needed.

As pointed out in the foreword of this book one out of
ten boys and one out of four girls are sexually victimized
as children. Some say the figure is higher than this but no
one really knows. If one looks at troubled populations such
as the mentally ill, the chemically dependent and criminals
(including sex offenders), the percentages of those sexually abused as children rises considerably.

In most cases abusers of children are known to them.
They are family members, teachers, church workers or
clergy, day care personnel, family "friends." The news of
a child being snatched off the street by a predatory
stranger gets the press but this scenario is the exception to
the rule.

Predators who are strangers present by far the greatest
danger to the life of the child. On the other hand sexual
abusers in the home or in the inner circle of the child's
world present the greatest danger of psychological damage
to the child.

Not all sexually abused children grow up to be socially dysfunctional even though the functional ability of all is impaired. Victims of incest can never enjoy a fully normal sexual relationships if any at all. The specter of mistrust and an uncontrolled, unsafe, environment haunts them for a lifetime.

Often the effects of the abuse are hidden under layers of psychological denial until later in life. A victim of childhood sexual abuse may not become floridly symptomatic until their twenties, thirties, or even later.

Suppressed memory is a common symptom of childhood sexual abuse. Missing years from childhood memories are not uncommon. Such losses of time can be symptomatic of problems other than sexual abuse. Problems such as illness, severe family problems, and other things.

Often victims of incest will act out at an early age, especially in adolescence. Unable to fully participate in normal adolescent social development they may play more bizarre roles involving things like drug addiction, gang activity, sexual acting out, or avoidance of normal adolescent sexual activity.

Normal activity for adolescents involves dating and otherwise socializing with peers. A child who has been sexually abused by his or her own parents or another adult is not going to engage in social activities normal for their age. The fourteen year-old girl who has been sexually assaulted by her father for five years is not apt to sit around with other girls giggling about boys.

In adolescence and later in the lives of sexually abused children symptoms such as nightmares, sleep disturbances, psychiatric disorders, dissociative disorders, suicidal ideation, rage, and many others manifest themselves.

A major life problem faced by victims of childhood sexual abuse is the inability to form object relations or any sort of relations with others which require any level of trust. People who are sexually abused as children have had their childhood stolen. They can never fully recover. A child who has been sexually abused by a relative or any adult can never experience normal sexual development as an adolescent and young adult. The learning experience has been ruined for them forever.

In addition to seeking ways of dealing with sex offenders themselves we need to continue seeking ways for people to avoid being victimized and to recover as much as possible if they have been victimized.

Strategies For Prevention

One way of coping with sexual abusers is to harden the target by helping children and adults develop coping skills to avoid sexual abuse. This is not to suggest that the victim is ever responsible for the offense behavior but potential victims can learn self-defense techniques and assume some responsibility for self-protection.

Sexual predators, like any other predator, seek out the easy target. A woman or child alone on a dark street or in broad daylight, the runaway teenager, children with dysfunctional parents, persons in a relationship involving high degrees of trust such as clergy, physicians, teachers.

Self-protection is quite problematic for children. Children should not feel an inordinate need to protect themselves from adults in their environment. Children have a need to feel free to explore the world at its fullest. Unfortunately, no matter what children are taught, pedophiles are highly skilled at breaking through their defenses.

Intensive screening of adults charged with the supervision of children is one way of protecting them. Another need is that institutions charged with the supervision of such adults be committed to careful supervision. Immediate action in situations where problems are suspected is called for.

An example of a major systemic failure was identified in the Roman Catholic Arch Diocese of Dallas-Fort Worth in Texas. After the arrest and conviction of a priest for the sexual abuse of many boys, the church was successfully sued for one hundred and twenty million dollars for its negligence in addressing the situation. Church officials ignored numerous complaints about the priest, who kept boys in his apartment overnight and violated all sorts of observable professional barriers.

Of course the Roman Catholic Church has no monopoly on sexual misconduct, even if it does appear to have been the most organized in defending the criminals and covering up the scandals.

Most, if not all, communities in the United States provide numerous resources for training in self-protection. Local police agencies, women's organizations, children's protective agencies, and schools should be able to furnish one with referral information on self-protection training. If these agencies in your community cannot provide such information you should demand that they do this.

Strategies For Survival

As stated throughout this book the problem of sexual assault is generally only dealt with after the crime has been committed. In view of this after-the-fact approach there are millions of suffering victims which need the help of others to survive the assaults with minimal damage to their lives.

Much can be done in the area of assisting victims in developing coping skills to deal with their victimization. This can be done prior to as well as after the assault. A few years ago the Boy Scouts Of America developed a video for young boys instructing them how to protect themselves from sexual assault and what to do if they are assaulted.

For many reasons deeply rooted in our culture child and adult victims of sexual assault are usually reluctant to seek help. Sexual assault is usually accompanied by a sense of shame and guilt on the part of the victim. In many cultures, and formerly in western society, victims of sexual assault were and still are punished.

The Judeo-Christian law as outlined in Deuteronomy calls for the execution of women raped in the city where it is assumed they could call out for help. It doesn't allow for being scared speechless or being bound and gagged. This law remains essentially in effect and enforceable in some Moslem societies today.

The idea of berating the victim was recently expressed by a television news anchor person who spoke of a young rape victim as having "lost her innocence." My calls to complain about what I considered a secondary assault on the child remain unanswered. I'm sure the news person meant no harm. Rape victims have long been thought of has having "lost their innocence." She just didn't think about what she was really saying. Perhaps she should have said "stolen" instead of "lost."

A victim of rape doesn't lose his or her innocence. They may have their peace of mind stolen by a criminal and they don't need to be instructed in what they may have lost. This same anchor person also referred to a child victim of a drive-by shooting as "being in the wrong place at the wrong time." It was midnight and the child was in bed. Wasn't it the criminal who was in the wrong place at the wrong time, doing the wrong thing ?

Like other thieves, sex offenders select their victims carefully. They do this for both their own pleasure and to minimize their chances of getting caught. The measures the offenders utilize to protect themselves often brutalize the victim as much as the assault itself.

One offender I treated preyed on young immigrant Hispanic women. He was himself from El Salvador and chose these women because he thought they would not report the offense. He believed they feared the police and other authority figures in the United States. He believed that a woman who had been raped was considered in some way damaged and therefore reluctant to make a report. Unfortunately for him this stereotyping did not hold up and one of his victims blew the whistle.

Children are especially vulnerable to pedophiles who warn them of the consequences of telling. Children do not have the experience to know whether the pedophile is telling the truth and fear rejection by their parents. They fear whatever consequences the pedophile promises. In some cases pedophiles threaten to harm the parents and this is especially terrifying.

Unfortunately children are sometimes ignored or berated when they report sexual abuse. This is especially common in the case of incest where disclosure can sometimes have disastrous social and economic consequences for the family. The mother, threatened by the loss of her husband and possibly his income, may be so invested in denial that she may reject her own child at the disclosure of incest.

In the previously mentioned case of the Dallas-Fort Worth Arch Diocese, church officials chose denial of the problem as a way of dealing with it. The Arch Diocese was subsequently sued for one hundred and twenty million dollars because of its cover-up of the situation and refusal to act in a responsible, and dare I say, Christian way.

Society should not hesitate to prosecute those who aid, comfort, conspire and otherwise support sex offenders. We should attack both the offenders and the social infrastructures which supports them. The responsible parties of the Arch Diocese ought to be tried for complicity in the violent acts they allowed to be committed against the children in their care. The priest who abused these children is not the only one who belongs in prison.

Persons who cover for their incestuous spouses should be held fully accountable for their part in the offense behavior. If the mother who accuses her sexually assaulted daughter of lying were also to face prosecution, she might consider alternative actions which might protect the child.

Supporters of sexual offenders also include police, court personnel, and others who ask rape victims questions like "what were you wearing?" (to incite the rapist), "what were you doing?" (to encourage the rapist). Provocative and irresponsible dress is an issue but it must always be treated as a separate issue from the crime of sexual assault. Part of the above suggested self-defense training should be training emphasizing the innocence of the victim. Victims and potential victims should be strongly encouraged to report their abuse.

To encourage reporting of sexual abuse potential victims need reassurance that they will not be punished for reporting. Particularly in the case of children, offenders will tell them they will get into trouble if they tell. At best such a disclosure of sexual victimization is an embarrassment. This shame, however irrational, is difficult to suppress.

Essentially all involved in sexual assault, including the perpetrator, are victims. This can and should be acknowledged, but all should also be held responsible for their part in the crime. If "co-offenders" were held responsible for their part in the crime (and they seldom are), sex offenders would begin losing their social supports. In addition these "co-offenders" can be forced to begin dealing with their problems, which are part of the pathological family and social systems that support sexual abuse.

In seeking recovery the victims of sexual assault have to deal with the damage done to them by family and social systems, by co-perpetrators as well as the perpetrator himself. Because of the nature of sexual assault, the victim is damaged in a very extensive way. The spouse of the offender, or police officer who blames the victim for the offense, may have done even more damage to the victim than the offender.

The hatred many rapists have for females comes from their mother's inability to protect them from assault. This hatred intensifies when the mother also blames them for the assault. We can blame the rapist all we wish for the way in which he expresses his anger, but until we acknowledge the source of this anger we will do little to prevent the development of this sort of pathology.

In long term psychotherapy many of the issues involved in victimization can be sorted out and worked on.

Many victims, however, do not have access to this costly process. Lack of resources is often a secondary result of the dysfunctional existence suffered by victims of sexual assault.

Where feasible, perpetrators should be required to pay for treatment, but this is generally not an option for someone in prison. If they can pay they should never be required to pay directly to the treatment provider or victim but to some third party designated by the court.

Self-help groups are available and a list of these are usually available through general crisis information lines and women's organizations. It is very helpful if these groups are used in conjunction with professional help. Self-help groups such as Alcoholics Anonymous, Narcotics Anonymous, and Overeaters Anonymous, when applicable, are good forums for exploring issues arising out of abuse.

Frequently victims of sexual assault suffer from mental problems including clinical depression and other mental illnesses. These victims may be highly suicidal and in general suffer from much higher rates of chemical dependency. Victims may be in life threatening crises so severe that long term therapy may not be an option at the time of problem identification. One of the young men abused in the Dallas-Fort Worth Arch Diocese case mentioned was driven to suicide by the experience.

Another block to long term treatment lies in the victims' fear of people and their inability to trust others. Also, deep issues of shame associated with the experience make self-disclosure very painful. Finally, feeling of rage and social isolation make working with treatment providers and others extremely difficult.

Victims desperately need whatever encouragement and support others can provide to engage in treatment. Treatment providers should be highly skilled in working with such victims. This work requires a very gentle touch, patience, and clinical skill in keeping the victim engaged in the process.

The reason for the gentle approach to the treatment of victims of sexual assault is that the process is so painful and frightening. The treatment itself is so traumatic the victim is driven to retreat into previous states of denial. It might be compared to the treatment of a person with severe orthopedic injuries who has to be forced out of the wheelchair to engage in painful rehabilitation.

Summary and Conclusions

In this book, I have tried to present several simple ideas regarding the problems of social functioning in general and sexual abuse in particular. These may be summarized as follows:

1. Profound technological, economic, and social changes in the last century have helped to create a situation in which many of society's structural and managerial mechanisms have undergone a diminished capacity to function. Specifically, the small community and family systems which once determined so much about how people lived have, to an extent, broken down.

2. Society has not been able to develop sufficient new social control mechanisms and this has led to a sort of social anarchy. This social state does provide individuals with many interesting new choices in life. While they are a wonderful development, these choices also lead to much confusion and social disorder as people work to develop criteria upon which to make them.

3. Children need of a long period of nurturing, protection and support by two parents even though society seems less and less able to provide this. More and more children are left to fend for themselves in broken and single parent homes without the extended family or close community supports of the past.

4. In general, all people are equipped with many physiological and social characteristics developed over millions of

years of human development. Many of these characteristics have a diminished function in today's world.

5. One symptom of the current state of social dysfunction is
a rise in the incidence of sexual dysfunction which
includes sexual assault.

6. In a effort to restore order society people have looked
more and more to the criminal justice system for solutions to such problems as sexual assault and chemical
dependency. While this system does offer some valuable
tools for social control, it is both end stage in its response
and limited in its applicability.

7. We are a society which tends turns a blind eye to healthy
social (including sexual) education and interaction and
obsesses on deviancy. All one has to do is to check out
the television talk shows or daily news items to know this
is true.

8. Society has the option of developing new or restoring
some old supportive institutions and reconnecting as a
society. We can start by recognizing that much of society
has already accomplished this and can provide valuable
models. How about a talk show entitled "Parents
Whose Children Don't Use Drugs" or "People Who
Finished College."

9. To an extent finding solutions to society's problems
depends on the willingness of people to go public find
ways of interacting in meaningful and positive ways.
One can not really get in touch with what is going on by
watching or reading the news. The news almost exclu-
sively focuses on the bizarre, the deviant, the violent
and, in general, that which has gone wrong in the world.

10. There is probably no way we can reconstruct the community and family systems of the past. In many cases we
would not want to. We must, however, find ways of

either changing the needs they once met or other ways of meeting those needs.

In the Appendices and Bibliographical sections of this book there are a number of references where additional information can be obtained. Working with your local civic groups, churches and other religious organizations, schools, child protective agencies, law enforcement agencies and other social organizations, we can identify (and many are identifying) problems. We can work to achieve solutions on a community level.

Glossary
Probation and Parole
Terminology

Division of Intensive Sanctions (DIS): An alternative to traditional prison confinement. DIS provides a program that is more restrictive than probation or parole, but less restrictive than traditional prison. Participants are treated as inmates. By Department of Corrections (DOC) policy, sex offenders may not be assigned to DIS.

DOJ: Department of Justice.

DOC: Department of Corrections.

DPP: Division of Probation and Parole.

Electronic Monitoring (EM): Used to monitor offenders in their homes. One part attached to the telephone, a second to the offender.

Felony: Criminal offense punishable by imprisonment. Many offenders convicted of felonies, however, never go to prison. Most crimes involving child victims are felonies.

Incest or Intra-Family Child Sexual Abuse: Any attempted or actual sexual behavior with a minor by a related adult (parent, grandparent, step-parent, live-in girlfriend or boyfriend, uncle, etc.); or with any minor by a related minor five or more years older than the victim.

MR: Mandatory Release

Misdemeanor: A criminal offense less than a felony. Many offenders convicted of misdemeanors never go to jail.

Parole: The release of a prisoner before a sentence has expired on condition of future good behavior. The sentence is not set aside; the offender remains under supervision.

Discretionary: The release of an eligible prisoner , at a point prior to the prisoner's Mandatory Release date.

Mandatory Release (MR): By statute, a prisoner must be released to parole supervision after serving a certain percentage of the sentence. First- or Second-Degree Sexual Assaults are among designated "serious" offenses.

Parole Eligibility Date (PED): The date at which a prisoner qualifies for review for possible release on parole. It is not a guaranteed release date.

PED: Parole Eligibility Date.

Pedophilia: The condition in which a child or adolescent is chosen as the primary sexual object.

Perpetrator: A person who commits an offense.

Probation: The suspension of sentence of a person convicted but not yet imprisoned, on condition of continued good behavior and compliance with special rules and conditions.

Recidivism: The reoccurrence of criminal behavior (repeat offenders).

Revocation of Probation or Parole: The removal of an offender from probation or parole supervision following a violation of court ordered conditions or rules of probation or parole supervision. The offender is returned to prison or to the sentencing court for imposition of a sentence.

Sex Offender Intensive Supervision (SO-ISP): A program to supervise sex offenders on probation or parole who pose the highest risk to the community

Sex Offender Registration: Upon discharge from probation or parole, offenders convicted of certain sex offenses must report their home addresses, place of employment or school, and employment duties to the Department of Justice. Updated information must be reported at least annually for fifteen years after discharge.

Sexual Assault: Anyone who has sexual contact or sexual intercourse with another person, without consent of that person, is guilty of sexual assault. Children under age 16 are presumed incapable of consenting to sexual activity.

Sexual Predator: A person previously convicted of a sexually violent offense who has a mental disorder which predisposes the person to engage in acts of sexual violence. The state may petition for a Civil Commitment when such an individual is within 90 days of release from custody

SO-ISP: Sex Offender-Intensive Supervision Program.

California's Megan's Law

Megan's Law is named after seven-year-old Megan Kanka, a New Jersey girl who was raped and killed by a known child molester who had moved in across the street from the Kankas — without their knowledge. Megan's parents embarked on a national crusade to change federal and state laws to allow for community notification of released sex offenders.

Ruling on N.J. sex offender again upholds Megan's Law

By THOMAS GINSBERG
Philadelphia Inquirer

PHILADELPHIA – A federal court in Philadelphia on Wednesday upheld communities' right to know if high-risk sex offenders live in their midst, delivering the country's most authoritative ruling yet on Megan's Laws and setting the stage for a possible appeal to the U.S. Supreme Court.

The ruling by the U.S. Court of Appeals for the Third Circuit in a New Jersey law cleared the way for notifications to begin in New Jersey in about a month, after being on hold for two years as lawyers battled over the statute, officials said

'The fundamental premise of Megan's Law is that registration and carefully tailored notification can enable law enforcement and those likely to encounter a sex offender to be aware of a potential danger and to stay vigilant against possible re-abuse.

Federal court ruling

are awaiting hearings, according to state Attorney General Peter Verniero.

Supporters welcomed Wednesday's ruling as a major step in a long

ruling the "most significant" yet on Megan's Laws.

"This is not punitive, it's regulatory ... and the decision of the court today certainly echoed that," he said.

Agencies of Interest

Office of Justice Programs

The Office of Justice Programs (OJP) works with federal, state and local agencies, and national and community-based organizations to develop criminal and juvenile justice programs. OJP, with its comprehensive approaches, operates under a mission is to provide federal leadership in developing the nation's capacity to prevent and control crime, administer justice and assist crime victims. Contact these agencies at the following address:

- Bureau of Justice Statistics (BJS)
- National Institute of Justice (NIJ)
- Office of Juvenile Justice & Delinquency Prevention (OJJDP)
- Office for Victims of Crime (OVC)

810 Seventh Street, N.W. Washington, DC 20531.
Telephone: 202 / 307-0703

Community Notification and Recidivism

NCIA Research Volunteers Draft

November 8th, 1996
quoted from Internet site
http://www.ncianet.org/ncia

"How should Community Notification be implemented? Who should have access to the information? Will notification be effective? Is it needed? Is it just? Is it constitutional? Do once caught sex offenders pose a high risk of re-offending, more so than murderers or other criminals? How do we know?

Is Community Notification the only way to deal with former sex offenders, as opposed to every other class of criminal? If so, how should notification be handled? Who should be told? Who, if anyone, should not be told? Does telling reduce or increase the risk of re-offense? Again, how do we know?

Whether the public labeling of sex offenders is socially effective, morally right, or even constitutional, there is no denying its popularity. It sells newspapers. It gets votes. Willie Horton, a sex offender and a true monster, helped elect a president.

Community Notification titillates and may even satisfy an enormous public appetite, but even its strongest advocates acknowledge that it comes with a price. Hate crimes. Public paranoia. Violence. Selective denial of human rights. Creation of a new criminal underclass.

But how many sex offenders are like Willie Horton? All of them? Most of them? To answer some of those questions, we have a very practical need to know how many offenders, once caught, will offend again.

In preparing its April 1996 Research Update, the National Center for Institutions and Alternatives reviewed a substantial public database of scientific studies related to sex offender treatment and recidivism. Based on that research, NCIA concluded that public policy in this area often is based on misinterpretations, bending of the facts, and myth.

Part of the problem has been the sheer number of studies that have accumulated over the past 50 years on the subject of sex offender recidivism. Until recently and the advent of more careful meta analysis comparisons, people had difficulty in sorting out the results.

"But maybe now," as Dr. Margaret Alexander pointed out, "through an accumulation of studies we can." Saying this in her Oshkosh Institution's November 1994 Report to the ASTA Conference, her team's "Quasi Meta-Analysis II" did just that. It evaluated an extensive number of sex offender studies, 673 of them, laboriously coding 74 to a standardized form.

Until a few months ago there had been but two really landmark evaluations that looked at most all of the hundreds of studies done to date. The impressive Oshkosh Correctional Institution's study and another voluminous overview in 1989 by Lita Furby, Mark Weinrott and Lyn

Blackshaw. Now however, just published in April 1996, we have still another major compilation, this one from Dr. R. Karl Hanson and Monique T. Bussiere of the Office of Canada's Solicitor General. Collectively between these three robust reviews, we may at last have a considerably less changeable accumulation of data that in total has tracked tens of thousands of sex offenders, many of them for lengthy periods of time.

As the focus of this paper is solely to address the issue of Community Notification, we culled these three compilations to look only at sex offenders who had once been caught.

We isolated these individuals because they have been identified to the authorities as sex criminals. Unidentified offenders are likely to have higher offense rates, but solid information cannot be known about their behavior because they are - by definition - unidentified.

Between these three reviews, over 800 new studies have now been marshaled. Most importantly, 207 of the studies specifically addressed rearrests for a subsequent sex offense, hereinafter referred to as "reafasso" rates....(Furby so enumerates in 37 studies, Alexander in 83 studies (68 + 15), and the Solicitor General in 87 usable documents).

When the "reafasso" rates are isolated from all these studies and properly weighted and interpolated, a recidivism figure is found which will be a surprise to most:

**With or without treatment,
the vast majority of once-caught sex offenders
87%
don't go on to be rearrested for a subsequent new
sex offense. Sex offender recidivism Is much lower
than people believe. Only a small minority**

13%
of those that community notification might confront go on to be rearrested for a subsequent new sex crime.

6,534	Alexander-Oshkosh Correctional Institution 1994 See attached Alexander bar graph (treateds only)	10.9%
1,219	Alexander-Oshkosh Correctional Institution 1994 See attached Alexander bar graph (untreateds only)	18.5%
15,361	Furby-Blackshaw-Weinrott 1989 See Our exhibit (B)	12.7%
23,393	Office of Canada's Solicitor General 1996 See Excerpt from their Executive Summary	13.4%
46,507	See our weighted average calculation Exhibit (C)	12.95%

Rounding 12.95% to 13% tells us that 87% 8.7 out of 10 once caught sex offenders do not go on to be rearrested for a new sex offense.

A word of caution...it should be noted that the total number of rearrested subjects, 46,507 counts some people twice because the Furby, Alexander and the Solicitor General's Office pulled from hundreds of studies, a few of which were the same studies.

In spite of that reification, what these recent reviews still leave us with is an immense data pool of the tracking of tens of thousands of sex offenders. Most notable...all three reviews, after accumulating from all the other studies provide nearly the same results. Collectively recidivism rates for a new sex offense are in the low teens.

Although the unearthing of a modest 13% recidivism rate for the once caught comes from years of research and hundreds of studies, few people are going to believe so few recidivate. But the fact is until other reviews come along, that accumulate even more data, that track even more subjects, this latest finding of 13% recidivism rate should not be dismissed.

When compared to other types of criminals, sex offenders also have a far lower rate of going back to jail. When criminologists compare sex offender recidivism to the F.B.I.'s 1994 statistic.... "that 74% of all of those released from prison" for all types of crime "are back in prison within four years"... a degree of how much mis- or dis-information we've heard begins to emerge.

Although any recidivism of a sexual nature is not to be minimized, the 1.3 out of 10 who are rearrested for a subsequent sex crime is a far cry from the 7.4 out of 10 who are being arrested and going back to prison for other types of crime.

Skewing Recidivism Rates

When being tough on crime and skewing recidivism rates remains one of their best vote getting ploys, politicians aren't about to shoot themselves in the foot acknowledging low re-offense rates. For them finding a study from somewhere with high recidivism rates has been easy. There are so many recidivism studies out there that a few can be found to say almost anything. When one hears of a study citing high re-offense rates, closer scrutiny will often however lead either to someone focused on the most serious offenders, or to some study with a minuscule data pool, that may have tracked only a couple of hundred subjects, or less.

Another way for spinmasters to disparage the findings of new research is to decree whatever comes along as "inconclusive." You will also hear "up to" figures: "up to 40% re-offend," "up to 75% re-offend." The trouble with such claims is they are not averages, and they are not backed by any credible broad base of data like the massive works of Alexander, Furby or Hanson.

Offense rates for some categories of offenders may be "up to" about 30%, but other categories may be "as low as" 3%. What matters is the average offense rate or a careful tracking of which offense rate fits which category. If one were to sample a group of sexually dangerous psychotics, a 100% recidivism rate might be conceivable, but the average sex offender is not in that psychosexually afflicted group.

One politician, Assemblyman Bill Hoge on the make in this last election in Pasadena was claiming without any credible basis whatsoever that sex offenders "will repeat the crime again at least 90% of the time." Frank Zimring a Law Professor at the University of California at Berkeley addressing Assemblyman Hoge has written "that such gross exaggerations are a folk belief, that what we are looking at is the dynamics of ignorance in action" that "this is don't bother me with the facts legislation."

Still another ruse in promoting the myth of high re-offense rates is to leave out the word *sexual* and cite the arrest rates of sex offenders for other types of crime. If a convicted sex offender later shoplifts, he has committed a new offense, but it's not a new *sex* offense.

But even by this measure, the arrest rates of sex offenders for other types of crime compare favorably with the arrest rates of others. If for accuracy you interpolate from large data pools, sex offenders get arrested for other types of crime (including probation violations) at about half the rate of other criminals.

Offense rates are very different before and after being caught. Although many sex offenders may offend for sometime before being apprehended, the commission of new offenses becomes considerably more difficult once they have been caught and are known to law enforcement. As later detailed in this paper, there are a number if reasons why once caught sex offenders become less likely to continue offending.

How Many Sex Offenders Are We Dealing With?

The total hasn't been tabulated yet. Depending on how far the states are legally allowed to go back in time (if they are allowed to go back), it looks like at least 250,000 will be affected.

According to the State of Washington's Institute for Public Policy, by the time of their July, 1996 review, 135,638 sex offenders had already registered themselves in the 50 states.

When you apply the finding that 87% do not go on to commit a new sex offense, what should be reflected upon is that once 250,000 have registered over 217,000 of those souls will be ex offenders.

To paint pretty much all with the same brush, to permanently label so many who won't again re-offend is not only unfair but a major injustice that will only compound the problem.

From the Perspective of the Ex-Offender

It is well established that most sex offenders have histories of being molested themselves as children. This trauma leaves many of them with a long term problem of clouded boundaries. If the problem becomes deep seated enough, the victim may become a perpetrator. But with arrest and the other shocking consequences of being discovered, those uncertain boundaries are suddenly and vividly redrawn. For most, that drawing emerges with very hard lines.

More than with any other class of offender, getting caught leaves sex offenders humiliated, shamed and shaken to the core. Being handcuffed and hauled away from decent society is a shattering experience for anyone, but it is all the more electrifying and soul-stripping when the nature of the offense is as intimate and shameful secret as is a sex crime. In some cases, the perpetrator's first real lesson in recognizing the consequence for his behavior comes with the shock of seeing his name and perhaps his picture in the newspaper or on television, accused and exposed before all his friends, family, neighbors, co-workers.

The process hardly ends with arrest. Prior to sentencing, which can sometimes take a year or more, little can be worse than the prolonged agonies and reflections of not knowing how long one may be going to prison, for some it may be for life. In this setting, life around them becomes narrow and terrifying. If pending trial, a sex offender is already bracketed in jail, it may be the first time his blurred boundaries come face to face with real vengeance. Greeted with beatings or worse, many first time sex offenders are startled by the degree of rage they now must encounter. Perhaps most devastating of all is the gradual realization that they are themselves criminals and as a known sex offender, the safety, comfort and security of the life left behind may be gone forever.

All of this is much more of a shock than putting a finger in a light socket, it is not just another passing experience. For sex offenders, more than almost any other class of criminal, being caught is the major crossroad in their lives. As with other forms of extreme aversion therapy, all of these humiliations imprint a painful, life-changing lesson. Few will ever forget the nightmare. As these low recidivism rates attest, getting caught teaches most.

Towards A Policy That Works

Widespread Community Notification that makes dartboards out of sex offenders is risky business. We shouldn't be damning people and we shouldn't be making an outcast or pariah of anyone. Setting any group up to be hassled, hunted or taunted, is not the way to have less crime.

Long term provocation of sex offenders could very well set up the very same anxieties, frustrations, depression and despair that may have precipitated or been a part of the cause of their deviant behavior in the first place.

Making life-time lepers out of most all sex offenders could cripple the recovery of many and irrevocably some. Such tramplings that make sport out of destroying people will most certainly not reduce re-offense rates, it only sets a stage for further irresponsibility.

If one is to become permanently tagged as a deviant criminal, just keeping a job, a home, a family becomes a problem.

Although society is fearful and has every right to be anguished, if we want fewer victims, the monitoring of such a complex problem should not be turned over to a public that is untrained, misinformed on recidivism and fixated more on punishment than on curing the problem.

Unless we're going back to the dark ages of our history, unless we're returning to a punishment mentality only, we should not be giving license to the kinds of Salem-like witch hunts that Community Notification is likely to encourage.

Permanent brandings may be all right for cattle, but it shouldn't be for people.

Treatment

Although many continue to question whether treatment works for sex offenders, it at the very least makes a great deal of difference. The April 1996 NCIA Research Update specifically addressed that question.

Those who say such behavior can't be modified might be reminded in very basic terms that pets get house trained, children get potty trained, and horses get ridden. Even animals from the wild can be taught to take direction at least in the circus. It is absurd to say that humans, the most intelligent of beings can't be realigned. Maybe the truly psychotic hard core can't be disciplined but they constitute a very minute fraction of sex offenders. As D. Thornton has written, "the results of a well designed and executed treatment program provides little support for the nihilistic belief that sexually aggressive behavior is irremediable." The majority of humans are capable of growth and achievement to maturity and sex offenders are no exception.

As the numbers in this paper show, a single arrest and probation cures most sex offenders even without treatment. However, over long periods of time recidivism rates do increase, but principally for those regarded as high risk. Accordingly, we should start demanding treatment of all sex offenders before and after release, with lengthy programs for some.

Without treatment a sex offender may never come to terms or realize the often devastating posttraumatic stress that he may have heaped upon a victim. For some victims, such stress if not treated, can cause a lifetime disorder. So treatment is needed for both the perpetrator and the victim not only for relief but as further insurance that it doesn't happen again.

The latest skills and techniques of relapse prevention are clearly proving themselves, particularly aversion therapies and those that develop victim empathy.

When the cost of treating sex offenders is a fraction of warehousing people in a debilitating cell, probational professionals trained in relapse prevention, would make a lot more sense than just building more prisons.

As we are soon to see more graduates from our prisons than from our colleges, we'd do well to think more of alternatives. There are other ways to fight crime, treatment is one of them. If our legislators truly want to do something constructive, they should start funding relapse prevention. With the latest regimens, such programs could well reduce recidivism into the low single digits.

If we're ever to deal more effectively, the actuality of low re-offense rates for the once caught should be acknowledged and treatment should be given more of a priority, more of a chance. If we want fewer victims of criminal sexual conduct, society must see past it's politicians and its resistance to rehabilitation.

Risk Assessments

Although most states are calling for risk assessments, i.e. low, moderate or high risk tiers, few ex offenders are likely to see a low risk assessment. Because of the lack of knowledge about these actual recidivism rates, most politically appointed Assessments Boards are likely to have serious qualms over assigning more than just a few sex offenders to a low risk tier. As a result, under most of the state notification laws, the general public will be given the addresses of almost all sex offenders.

One particularly well thought of expert in the field is Robert Freeman-Longo of The Safer Society Foundation. On risk assessments he writes:

> "The most serious problem in determining the dangerousness of a particular offender is the fact that there is no reliable risk checklist, risk assessments may be conducted by untrained persons using a standardized list of risk criteria. In the absence of highly qualified, trained professionals to conduct comprehensive risk assessments, the chance of miscalculated risk is increased."

Poorly or hastily researched risk assessments done by state boards or prosecutors will lead only to more problems. As all the studies in this paper attest, most sex offenders will never re-offend again, so if there is to be risk assessments, if the program is done fairly and professionally, most offenders should be assessed to a low risk tier. As that is not likely, the whole costly program may very well become bogus and a sham. In this set up, most offenders are likely to be painted with the same barbaric brush as if wearing the Scarlet Letter A. Once so damned, they and their families could well be hounded for the rest of their lives.

Registration

Sex offenders, would object less to registering if that information was to be kept relatively private. Some of the states have prudently decided such information shall only be available to law enforcement. Sex offenders do feel, however, that registering and re-registering every year or every 90 days or whenever they move, for periods like 15 to 25 years or for life is an overreaction, a painful burden, a singling out and overkill.

There are also complaints of excessive penalties for not registering and very short time frames to do so. Many states now require registry within 5 days or even 48 hours—and not just if one is moving to the state. Nevada and Florida have gone so far as to say sex offenders "must register within 48 hours of entering." In these states, even passing through could land one in jail. The penalty is as much as a year in jail in Nevada. In Florida, it's worse. Failing to register within 48 hours is a felony.

Under the soon-to-be imposed Federal identification program, the penalty for not registering has been propelled to a base fine of $100,000.

Particularly onerous to ex-offenders are also the *ex post facto* and *double jeopardy* attempts by the states to impose what are in effect new sentences. Some are trying to scoop up in their registries all sex offenders, even though many have completed their sentences decades ago. Until now and these new enactments, their debts to society had supposedly been paid.

As the vast majority of once caught sex offenders are not re-offending, little is served by their having to near endlessly register and reregister. Before any such extra punishment is allowed to stand, legislators should be made to prove their claims of high re-offense rates. If they can not, both new laws Community Notification and Registration should be struck down.

This situation is analogous to legislation, which is sometimes overturned because it is too broad. For example, in October 1996 a juvenile curfew in D.C. was overturned in Federal Court because of flawed statistics. The judge did so citing that although the city had a compelling interest to reduce juvenile crime, it passed the legislation without credible statistical evidence that there was more crime at night or that the curfew would primarily reach children likely to commit crimes. In the absence of credible statistical evidence that once caught sex offenders pose a high risk of re-offense, should not Community Notification and Registration Laws not be similarly overturned? Regardless of popular belief, if the statistics of our politicians are flawed, if indeed the allegation of a high re-offense rate is false, these new laws should not be allowed to continue on the books.

Will Community Notification Be Effective ?

For a number of reasons it won't be. One of the more obvious is the fact that if someone is still offending, and is known in his neighborhood as a sex offender, there's little to stop him from traveling a short distance to some other neighborhood where he is not known.

Couple this with the fact that 95 some percent of child molestation is said to take place in the home, by a family member or close friend, until that party is caught, that problem will not be addressed by anything as simplistic as a neighborhood sex offender watch. Such legislation may feel good, but it will do very little to stop the real problem.

What's confusing to a community is that when they are told of a sex offender's presence, 87% of that notification is irrelevant. The offender has already been punished—sometimes years before—and none in that 87% group will go on to be rearrested for a subsequent sex offense.

Branding all identically with the few who will re-offend is where the damage comes in and not just to the former offender but often to his entire family. It may even cause further public pain for the victim.

Some will argue that distinctions between those who will re-offend and those who won't are too subtle for trained professionals to forecast reliably. If so, the logic of Community Notification would leave responsibility for that same judgment to a neighbor or the general public most of whom have had no training in these matters at all. This is not a solution; it is simply passing the buck on an emotionally charged issue that almost every politician finds too hot to handle.

Hate Crimes & Other Punishments

Even though Community Notification has as yet to be fully unleashed, there has already been some vigilantism. Today, released sex offenders are being greeted with slurs and sometimes slugs. Some have been beaten. Some have had their houses torched. One man found his dog decapitated, its head propped on his stoop.

If under Community Notification there's to be access to most all sex offenders, regardless of risk level, if virtually any hot head can get directed via 800 or 900 telephone directories to the home of most any sex offender, serious problems will abound...and not only for the offender, but for his family or who ever else may live with him. Where a sex offender is domiciled or may have lived in the past may even effect the value of the real estate. If that address remains in a directory, even the next owner may be targeted. What if a known sex offender lives next door? Even just being a neighbor might make it pretty hard to sell one's own house.

Many would like to inflict their own brand of punishment or just deserts on any rotten apple sex offenders they can find, and many will take that second bite if Community Notification gives them a near license to do so. One young sex offender hid in an upstairs closet petrified as he heard his family below get seriously pummeled in their own living room. In that incident, the enraged hot heads who had barged in were a father and son team, one of them was a Corrections Officer.

Headlines of tragic cases prompt a lot of bona fide anger but passing out sex offender addresses may become like dropping matches on oil soaked rags. If one wanted more crime, there may not be a better prescription than Community Notification.

Very few people other than some researchers and criminologists have ever heard that the vast majority of sex offenders, once-caught, do not go on to re-offend. So it's no wonder there's so much fear and anguish among the public. A lot of it, we suspect, may be because so many in our society have been victimized themselves.

Given this context, the public will find it difficult to accept the fact that re-offense rates are really low. The problem though remains, that if society wants fewer victims, it shouldn't be just other types of criminals who are given a peaceful path to realign. Once anyone has served his time for a crime, that should be it.

Although many will disbelieve the 13% recidivism mean found from all these studies, skeptics might consider this. Even if one were to double that 13% mean and called it 26%, the conclusion would be the same...the vast majority, even in that stretch...74% would still not be going on to be rearrested for a new sex crime.

When claims are made that registration is not extra punishment, that's certainly not what is being said and felt by the hundred of thousands of sex offenders who are now under the threat of heavy fines and or jail if they don't register. One sex offender who didn't register in California under their "three strikes and you're out" is now facing 25 years to life.

In one recent case in Virginia, after the community was notified of the presence of a teenage sex offender, the threats and hassles became so great for a mother that she told her son, that he had to move out. Now he's on the street without any family support. What's that prognosis? The odds are certainly not now better for that young man's recovery. Thanks to Community Notification, predicaments like this only insure the likelihood of more criminal conduct not less.

If through Community Notification we're going to make more difficult the road to redemption, we'll ultimately have only more victims to show for it. If the courts can't find the decency to rule some for the hundreds of thousands of souls who are not re-offending, then most importantly it must be done for the sake of fewer future victims.

Although giving sex offenders additional punishments maybe politically seductive, it eats away at the very footings of our Constitution.

Our forefathers protected all of us—not just some of us—against *ex post facto* laws and double jeopardy because such are inherently unfair, subject to uneven application, and fundamentally abusive. Like sex crimes, such measures violate the constitutional contract that holds together our society. But unlike the recidivism rates for the great majority of once caught sex offenders, laws once enacted go on virtually forever.

The claim that registration is not an extra punishment is proven false by the fears and renewed shame experienced by the hundreds of thousands of Americans suddenly under the threat of heavy fines or the penitentiary if they don't comply with a requirement that didn't exist at the time of their sentence.

Fear and shame are powerful silencers, not only for the recovering sex offenders but for their families who are the totally innocent victims of these new laws. The Safer Society writes, "is it fair to have others stare and gossip about people because they are married to a sexual offender or they are the sister, brother, parent or relative of the offender?" Community Notification will clearly not only punish offenders but entire families.

It is bad government that panders to the impulse for revenge, enacts laws through intimidation, or ignores the fearful silence of sex offenders and their families.

Consider everything that is actually involved in being inscribed on the roll of public shame, in reporting every year or every 90 days or with every move or in some states whenever you travel into the state, and doing so endlessly for decades or for an entire lifetime. How can we ask a former offender to shed the errors of the past if we make permanent the stigma that goes with them?

Unless one has lived through a lengthy period of probation or parole as a sex offender, it's hard to imagine the humiliation of repeatedly and forever reporting to define yourself to others in terms of past behavior that in almost every case has its roots in a tragedy of childhood. For the most fragile, those most in need of a better self image, support and encouragement, the near endless process of registering and re-registering will not add to the cure.

As most states are trying to reach back and require all sex offenders to register even though they may have offended many years ago, what has been served up is nothing less than an ex post facto extension of probation. What it amounts to is a new decades long or life sentence of parole. Not calling it an extra sentence or extra punishment may be very popular but it's preposterous.

It's been amazing to see how the public has been duped into thinking that the once caught sex offender isn't already registered. To claim sex offenders are not already known to law enforcement is a joke. Whether convicted or not, if one has ever been arrested for a sex offense, he has been photographed and fingerprinted and those records have been going from the local police and state police to the FBI for decades. There are few sex offenders who don't have to face parole or probation after their release from jail and generally they must report their whereabouts for 5, 10 or more years. Regardless of how long ago a sentence, those records remain. The debate we're now having is who should have those records. If we are to be prudent, we will keep such in the hands of law enforcement and probational professionals. To do otherwise is reckless.

Privacy

All who have done their time and served their sentences should be afforded some privacy. If they can't be granted that, it will be all the more difficult for them to maintain healthy emotions. Without some time and space, away from notoriety, free from constant stress and anxiety, the probability that an offender will turn to crime again is increased, not reduced.

Is some privacy for sex offenders really too much to ask? Few could care less if some perverts are getting a bad rap, but if in truth most the once caught are not re-offending, if in fact their threat to society has been vastly exaggerated, then there is no "emergency" for this type of legislation, and privacy should not be denied.

Even though these are not compassionate times and even though it may be politically too humane, poorly thought out legislation that forfeits or permanently takes privacy away from anyone, even sex offenders, is a serious erosion of liberty that undermines the very integrity of our judicial system.

Supreme Court Justice Louis Brandeis once wrote "The right to the left alone is the most comprehensive of right and the right most valued by civilized man."

In spite of that at least one state, New Jersey, has upheld Megan's law although even there it is now under a temporary restraining order. Many other states however have been more judicious and declared Community Notification unconstitutional. Among them - Alaska, Arizona, Illinois, New Hampshire and now most recently New York.

When psychologists and criminologists alike feel that Community Notification is more apt to propel re-offense than to reduce them, sanity will have to come from the courts as it certainly isn't coming from our politicians.

What Walter Dickey, a University of Wisconsin law professor, recently had to say about other rush to punishment laws also applies to Community Notification. He said, it is "designed to get people to think that it will take repeat offenders off the street, it tricks people into thinking the problem has been solved." The truth is that Community Notification and Registration has been legislated "not because it's good crime control but because it's good politics."

If our courts would recognize all this vote-crazed legislation for what it is, there could be a more civilized approach and less criminal sexual conduct as a result. Once our judges are apprised that Community Notification has been brought to us on a false premise, and that re-offense rates have been exaggerated, maybe we can go on to more intelligently deal with this painful social problem.

Community Notification and onerous decades long Registration laws are ill concocted, election-year lawmaking, and poor public policies. The electorate deserves better protection than laws that should be declared unconstitutional, and the legislative process is poorly served by a herd response that comes mostly from fear and scapegoating.

The legitimate, realistic goal of protecting innocent lives is better served by careful thought, fairness and the truth.

Before there is story after story of vigilantism, before thousands of souls and their innocent families become taunted and hounded, our courts must come forth more wisely and honestly then have our politicians.

Community Notification is contraindicated...it needs to be rethought...it needs to be put in check."

1 Bureau of Justice Statistics, Correctional Populations in the United States, 1992, p.53.

2 Federal Bureau of Investigation, Uniform Crime Reports, Crime in the United States, 1993, p.217.

3 Bureau of Justice Statistics, Correctional Populations in the United States, 1992, p.53, 54.

4 Bureau of Justice Statistics, National Corrections Reporting Program, 1992, pp.31, 38, 43.

5 Margaret Alexander, Sex Offender Treatment: A Response to Furby, et al 1989 Quasi Meta-Analysis, paper presented at conference of the American Association for the Treatment of Sexual Abusers, November 11, 1994, Figure 2.

6 Bureau of Justice Statistics, Recidivism of Prisoners Released in 1983, p.6.

7 Lita Furby, Mark Weinrott, Lyn Blackshaw, Sex Offender Recidivism: A Review, Psychological Bulletin, Volume 105, p.3, 1989.

8 Margaret Alexander, Sex Offender Treatment: A Response to Furby, et al 1989 Quasi Meta-Analysis, paper presented at ATSA conference, November 11, 1994.

9 Ibid., Figure 2.

10 Vermont Department of Corrections, Facts and Figures: Legislative Presentation, January 1995, p.85.

Parole & Probation Statistics

U.S. Department Of Justice
Media Release
February 2, 1997 from the Internet site
http://www.ojp.usdoj.gov/bjs/pub/press/soo.pr

SIXTY PERCENT OF CONVICTED SEX OFFENDERS ARE ON PAROLE OR PROBATION

Rapes and Sexual Assaults Decline WASHINGTON, D.C. -- According to a report released today by the Justice Department's Bureau of Justice Statistics (BJS), on any given day in 1994, almost 60 percent of the 234,000 convicted sex offenders under the care, custody or control of corrections officials in the United States were on parole or probation. An estimated 99,300 offenders convicted of rape or sexual assault were in local jails or state or federal prisons, while an estimated 134,300 convicted offenders were under conditional supervision in the community, such as parole (following imprisonment) or probation. (On average for all offenders, there are almost three offenders on probation or parole supervision in the community for each offender in jail or prison. However, for those convicted of rape or sexual assault, the ratio of those on conditional release to those incarcerated is 1.4 to 1.)

Sex offenders represent 4.7 percent of the almost 5 million convicted offenders serving time in federal or state prisons, or jails or on probation or parole. They comprise 1 percent of the federal prison population, 9.7 percent of the state prison population, 3.4 percent of the nation's jail inmates, 3.6 percent of the offenders on probation and 4 percent of the offenders on parole.

The BJS report, "Sex Offenses and Offenders," provides a comprehensive overview of current knowledge about the incidence and prevalence of rape and sexual assault, the characteristics of the victims and perpetrators and the response of the justice system to these crimes. The report draws on more than two dozen statistical programs maintained by BJS and the *Uniform Crime Reporting Program* of the Federal Bureau of Investigation.

It is the first national estimate of the size of the convicted sex offender population under the jurisdiction of federal, state and local correctional authorities. Declines in rape and sexual assault. According to BJS's *National Crime Victimization Survey*, which obtains rape and sexual assault information from both males and females, the number of rapes and sexual assaults reported by victims in 1995 declined significantly from the number reported by victims in 1993. The nation's residents 12 years old and older reported one rape or other violent sexual assault for every 624 men and women in the country during 1995. Two years earlier, the rate of violent sexual victimization was one for every 435 residents. In 1995 the rate of rape among women was 10 percent lower than in 1990. In addition, 97,000 rapes were recorded by law enforcement agencies in 1995, the lowest number since 1989 and the lowest rate per capita since 1985. Data are unavailable for other sex offenses.

During 1994 and 1995, only a third of the rape and sexual assault victims said they reported the offense to a law enforcement agency. In 1995 law enforcement agencies reported 34,650 arrests for forcible rape and 94,500 arrests for other sex offenses. There were 50 arrests for rape and other sex offenses per 100,000 United States residents. Children and teenagers are victims Per capita rates of rape and sexual assault are highest among young men and women 16 to 19 years old, urban residents, and low-income residents. There is no significant difference in the rate of rape or sexual assault on the basis of race. Data from police-recorded incidents of rape in three states showed that 44 percent of rape victims were younger than 18 years old, and two-thirds of violent sex offenders serving time in state prisons said their victims were younger than 18.

An estimated 15 percent of imprisoned rapists and 45 percent of those sentenced to prison for other sexual assaults (statutory rape, forcible sodomy and molestation) said their victims were 12 years old or younger. Most imprisoned sex offenders knew their victims. Among rapists, about 30 percent said their victims had been strangers, and of those convicted of other sexual assaults, less than 15 percent said the victims were people with whom they had no prior relationship. About two-thirds of the rapes and sexual assaults reported by victims in the BJS survey occurred between 6 p.m. and 6 a.m. Almost 60 percent took place in the victim's home or at the home of a friend, relative or neighbor.

Recidivism rates for sex crimes are higher among sex offenders.

Prior BJS follow-up studies of sex offenders discharged from prison or sentenced to probation showed that they have a generally lower rate of rearrest than other violent offenders but are substantially more likely than other violent offenders to be rearrested for a new violent sex offense. For example, approximately 8 percent of 2,214 rapists released from prisons in 11 states in 1983 were rearrested for a new rape within three years, compared to approximately 1 percent of released prisoners who served time for robbery or assault. Released rapists were found to be 10.5 times as likely as non-rapists to be rearrested for rape. Offenders who served time for sexual assault were 7.5 times as likely as those convicted of other crimes to be rearrested for a new sexual assault.

Report (NCJ-163392) was written by BJS statistician Lawrence A. Greenfeld.

Additional BJS materials may be obtained from the BJS fax-on-demand (301/251-5550) or calling the BJS Clearinghouse on 1-800/732-3277. Information about the Justice Department's Violence Against Women programs may be obtained on the Internet at

http://www.ojp.usdoj.gov/VAWGO BJS97003.

Bibliography

Americans Behind Bars: The International Use Of Incarceration, 1992-1993 By Marc Mauer, Assistant Director, The Sentencing Project, September 1994, 918 F Street NW Washington, Suite 501, Washington, D.C. 20004, 202-628-0871.

Bureau of Justice Statistics, Correctional Populations in the United States, 1992.

Federal Bureau of Investigation, Uniform Crime Reports, Crime in the United States, 1993.

Bureau of Justice Statistics, Correctional Populations in the United States, 1992.

Bureau of Justice Statistics, National Corrections Reporting Program, 1992.

Bureau of Justice Statistics, Recidivism of Prisoners Released in 1983.

Furby, Lita and Mark Weinrott, Lyn Blackshaw, *Sex Offender Recidivism: A Review*, Psychological Bulletin, Volume 105, 1989.

Hazelwood, Robert, MS. *The Serial Rapist-His Characteristics And Victims (Part 1).* Federal Bureau Of Investigation, U.S. Department Of Justice, Law Enforcement Bulletin, January-February 1989.

Hobbs, Frank and Laura Lippman. *Children's Well-Being: An International Comparison: International Population Report Series.* U.S. Department Of Commerce, Bureau Of Census 1990.

Quasi Meta-Analysis, paper presented at conference of the American Association for the Treatment of Sexual Abusers, November 11, 1994.

Index

A

abortion 19
Abraham 17
act out 26
age differential 36
age of consent 36
age of majority 36
alcoholism 58
American Psychiatric Association's Diagnostic Criteria 46
Amnesty, Incorporated 67
angels 18
anti-sex education 26
Archdiocese of Dallas-Ft. Worth 64

B

Bar Mitzvah 37
beauty contests 9, 44
being known as a victim of sexual abuse 10
Benet-Ramsey 44
betrayer 11
blame 15
blaming 38
breakdown of order in the family 59
Buddha 12

C

California 2
Canada 27
cause of sexual misbehavior 59
child development 1
child pornography 45
child support 7
Children's Protective Services 14
Chinatown 24, 61
Christ 12
clerical celibacy 64
commitment 41
community 60
community systems 8
confusion 10
consenting adults 35
conviction 3
co-offender 9
cope 11
correctional sex offender treatment program 59
crimes without victims 36
criminal codes 24
criminal justice 5
cult of the individual 15

D

date rape 10, 38
dead babies 58
degenerating American family system 8
denial 9, 43
Deuteronomy 10
devalued 10
developmental needs 58
deviant families 23
deviant groups 25